TRUE FACTS THAT SOUND LIKE Bull$#*t

NATURE

500 WILD FACTS FROM THE ZANIEST CORNERS OF THE WORLD

SHANE CARLEY

CIDER MILL PRESS

BOOK PUBLISHERS

13-Digit ISBN: 978-1-40034-147-4
10-Digit ISBN: 1-40034-147-7

This book may be ordered by mail from the publisher. Please include $5.99 for postage
and handling. Please support your local bookseller first!

Books published by Cider Mill Press Book Publishers are available at special discounts for
bulk purchases in the United States by corporations, institutions, and other organizations.
For more information, please contact the publisher.

Cider Mill Press Book Publishers
"Where good books are ready for press"
501 Nelson Place
Nashville, Tennessee 37214

cidermillpress.com

Typography: Adobe Caslon Pro, Festivo Letters No1,
Capriccio, Microbrew One, Trade Gothic LT Std
Illustrations by Rebecca Pry

Printed in the United States of America
24 25 26 27 28 VER 5 4 3 2 1
First Edition

[CONTENTS]

[Introduction]

A snowflake the size of a basketball. A mushroom that bleeds. A frog that breaks its bones in self-defense. You'll learn about all of these and more in *True Facts That Sound like Bull$#*t: Nature*, a book that celebrates the weird and wonderful world we call home. You'll learn about fiery craters that have been burning for decades. You'll learn about lightning bolts that stretch for hundreds of miles. You might even learn some unsettling things about your own body. Did you know that humans produce almost two quarts of mucus a day? It's true!

This book contains 500 facts about incredible animals, extreme weather, and underwater miracles. It presents facts about deadly diseases, frightening fungi, and ridiculous rocks. If you think you know everything there is to know about nature, think again! The only predictable thing about nature is that it is unpredictable, and you're sure to find something in these pages that will change the way you think about the world around you. So buckle up, open your mind, and enjoy the ride!

[Animals]

If you've ever seen a platypus, you already know that nature can be pretty weird. But the truth is, nature is even stranger than you think. Did you know that wombats poop cubes? Or that sloths only poop once per week? Don't worry—not every fact in this book is poop related, but it turns out that Mother Nature has a real sense of humor when it comes to bodily functions. In this section, you'll learn about animals that can survive in space, animals that have far, far too many teeth, and animals with deeply unfortunate names. It will change the way you look at the world around you!

1. THERE IS A TYPE OF SPIDER KNOWN AS THE "BIRD DUNG SPIDER" THAT CAN MIMIC THE SIZE, SHAPE, AND COLOR OF BIRD FECES.

2. THERE ARE OVER 6,000 SPECIES OF "JUMPING SPIDERS," WHICH CAN JUMP SIGNIFICANT DISTANCES. GOOD LUCK SLEEPING TONIGHT!

3. THERE ARE APPROXIMATELY 110 TRILLION MOSQUITOES ON THE PLANET EARTH—WHICH MEANS THAT THERE ARE ROUGHLY 13,000 MOSQUITOES PER HUMAN.

4. RESEARCHERS BELIEVE THAT CHICKENS WERE ORIGINALLY DOMESTICATED NOT FOR FOOD, BUT FOR COCKFIGHTING.

5. THE AVERAGE ROOSTER'S CROW CAN REACH 130 DECIBELS—WHICH IS ROUGHLY THE SAME NOISE LEVEL AS A JET ENGINE.

6. THE AVERAGE SNAIL HAS OVER 10,000 TEETH.

7. ALTHOUGH SPIDER SILK IS WIDELY CONSIDERED THE STRONGEST NATURAL MATERIAL, SNAIL TEETH ARE BELIEVED BY SOME SCIENTISTS TO BE EVEN STRONGER.

8. MAYFLIES HAVE SUCH SHORT LIFE SPANS THAT THEY HAVE NOT EVOLVED A FUNCTIONING DIGESTIVE SYSTEM.

9. DESPITE THEIR WHITE APPEARANCE, POLAR BEARS HAVE JET-BLACK SKIN UNDERNEATH.

10. POLAR BEARS ACTUALLY DON'T EVEN HAVE WHITE FUR; THEIR FUR IS TRANSLUCENT AND APPEARS WHITE BECAUSE OF THE WAY LIGHT SCATTERS THROUGH THE HOLLOW INTERIOR OF EACH HAIR.

11. WHILE THEY REMAIN A POPULAR TARGET FOR POACHERS, RHINOCEROS HORNS ARE ACTUALLY COMPOSED OF KERATIN—THE SAME MATERIAL YOUR FINGERNAILS ARE MADE FROM.

12. A 2017 SURVEY CONDUCTED BY THE INNOVATION CENTER FOR US DAIRY FOUND THAT 7% OF THE US POPULATION BELIEVES THAT CHOCOLATE MILK COMES FROM BROWN COWS.

13. WORKER BEES FLY A COMBINED TOTAL OF APPROXIMATELY 55,000 MILES (8,8514 KILOMETERS) TO GENERATE ONE POUND (ABOUT HALF A KILOGRAM) OF HONEY.

14. SOME SPECIES OF BATS ARE CAPABLE OF FLYING AT SPEEDS OF OVER 100 MPH (161 KMH)!

· 15 ·

WHEN A ROOSTER THROWS ITS HEAD BACK TO CROW, ITS EAR CANALS CLOSE TO MUFFLE THE SOUND AND PREVENT THE ROOSTER FROM DEAFENING ITSELF.

16. A STUDY RELEASED IN 2022 INDICATES THAT SPIDERS MAY HAVE DREAMS.

17. AFRICAN BUFFALO MAKE DECISIONS FOR THE HERD BY "VOTING." SPECIFICALLY, THEY ORIENT THEIR BODIES IN THE DIRECTION THEY WOULD LIKE THE HERD TO MOVE.

18. SLOTHS ONLY POOP ONCE PER WEEK.

19. THE IBERIAN RIBBED NEWT USES ITS OWN RIBS AS WEAPONS, PUSHING THEM THROUGH THE SKIN TO "STING" ATTACKERS WITH THE SPECIAL POISON THAT COATS THEM.

20. BURROWING OWLS ARE KNOWN FOR THEIR ABILITY TO RE-CREATE THE HISSING SOUND OF A RATTLESNAKE, USED AS A DEFENSE MECHANISM TO WARN OFF PREDATORS.

21. RECENTLY, SCIENTISTS HAVE DISCOVERED A GROUP OF BUTTERFLIES WITH UNIQUE MARKINGS ON THEIR WINGS—RESEMBLING THE FLAMING EYE OF SAURON FROM *THE LORD OF THE RINGS*—AND THEY HAVE BEEN NAMED SAURONA BUTTERFLIES IN TOLKIEN'S HONOR.

22. MANY PEOPLE BELIEVE THAT DOGS ARE COLOR-BLIND, BUT THIS ISN'T EXACTLY TRUE.

In reality, dogs can only perceive the colors blue and yellow.

23. GOATS HAVE "ACCENTS"—AND THOSE ACCENTS CAN CHANGE OVER TIME, BASED ON THE SOCIAL GROUP THE GOAT IS CURRENTLY WITH.

24. DOLPHINS HAVE BEEN TRAINED TO JUMP AS HIGH AS 26 FEET (NEARLY 8 METERS) ABOVE THE WATER!

25. MOST PEOPLE KNOW A GROUP OF CROWS IS CALLED A MURDER, BUT DID YOU KNOW THAT A GROUP OF PARROTS IS CALLED A PANDEMONIUM?

26. REINDEER EYES CHANGE COLOR THROUGHOUT THE YEAR. DURING THE SUMMER MONTHS, THEY ARE A YELLOW/GOLD COLOR, BUT IN THE WINTER, THEY FADE TO BLUE.

These changes help the reindeer see better in different light levels.

27. BARN OWLS HAVE EVOLVED TO PRODUCE SPECIAL FEATHERS THAT ALLOW THEM TO FLY ALMOST COMPLETELY SILENTLY, MAKING THEM INCREDIBLY EFFECTIVE PREDATORS.

· 28 ·

**WOMBAT POOP IS
CUBE SHAPED.**

• 29 •

THE COLOSSUS PENGUIN IS NOW EXTINCT, BUT MEMBERS OF ITS SPECIES ONCE STOOD NEARLY 7 FEET (OVER 2 METERS) TALL.

30. A POLAR BEAR CAN HOLD BETWEEN 15% AND 20% OF ITS BODY WEIGHT IN ITS STOMACH AT ANY GIVEN TIME.

That's a lot to digest.

31. RABBITS DON'T NATURALLY EAT CARROTS—OR ANY ROOT VEGETABLES, FOR THAT MATTER.

Blame Bugs Bunny for that myth.

32. WHEN A FEMALE FERRET GOES INTO HEAT, IT WILL DIE IF IT DOES NOT MATE.

33. BEFORE MATING, MALE PORCUPINES URINATE ON FEMALE PORCUPINES.

This sounds gross (and it is), but it serves an important biological function, signaling the female that it is time to mate.

34. IF A LESS-DESIRABLE ROOSTER MATES WITH A CHICKEN, THE CHICKEN IS CAPABLE OF EJECTING UP TO 80% OF THE UNWANTED SPERM.

35. HOMOSEXUALITY IS FAIRLY COMMON IN THE ANIMAL KINGDOM.

For example, approximately one in 12 sheep demonstrates a preference for same-sex intercourse.

36. ALBATROSS MATE FOR LIFE...BUT THEY CHEAT!

When separated from their social partners, albatross will often mate with others.

37. GOLDFINCHES ARE NOT ALWAYS GOLD.

During the winter, they fade to a pale gray color.

38. THE "ALPHA WOLF" IS A MYTH.

Researchers have only observed the emergence of a dominant male among captive wolves—never in nature.

39. THANKS TO THE DESIGN OF THEIR DIGESTIVE TRACT, RABBITS ARE INCAPABLE OF VOMITING.

40. RABBITS LICK EACH OTHER NOT JUST OUT OF AFFECTION, BUT AS A SIGN OF DOMINANCE.

41. THE AVERAGE FLEA CAN JUMP 8 INCHES (20 CENTIMETERS), WHICH DOESN'T SOUND THAT IMPRESSIVE...UNTIL YOU CONSIDER THAT 8 INCHES IS ROUGHLY 200 TIMES THE SIZE OF A FLEA'S BODY.

· 42 ·

MALE TURKEYS CAN FLOCK
TOGETHER AND TAKE ON THE
ROLE OF "WINGMEN"
TO SUPPORT THE MATING
EFFORTS OF THE GROUP'S
DOMINANT TOM BY SCARING
OFF OTHER POTENTIAL SUITORS
OR EVEN SERVING AS BACKUP
DANCERS WHEN A FEMALE
TURKEY IS IN VIEW.

· 43 ·

RATS ARE TICKLISH
AND WILL "LAUGH" IF
YOU TICKLE THEM.

44. CIVET IN ASIA ENJOY EATING COFFEE CHERRIES, AND THE CHERRIES FERMENT AS THEY PASS THROUGH THE CIVET'S DIGESTIVE SYSTEM.

Humans later collect the semidigested cherries and use them to brew a special coffee called kopi luwak—which is considered a delicacy. How adventurous are you feeling?

45. A CAT WAS ELECTED MAYOR OF THE ALASKAN TOWN OF TALKEETNA...

and held the position for 20 years!

46. GIRAFFES, CAMELS, AND CATS ARE THE ONLY ANIMALS THAT WALK BY MOVING BOTH LEGS ON ONE SIDE OF THEIR BODY, FOLLOWED BY BOTH LEGS ON THE OTHER SIDE.

47. PARROTS ARE KNOWN FOR THEIR ABILITY TO LEARN TO SPEAK WORDS, BUT ONE INCREDIBLE PARROT NAMED PUCK LEARNED A RECORD 1,728 WORDS DURING ITS LIFE.

48. THE LARGEST WORM IN THE WORLD IS THE GIANT GIPPSLAND EARTHWORM, WHICH CAN REACH LENGTHS OF NEARLY 10 FEET (3 METERS)!

49. OWLS DON'T HAVE EYEBALLS—THEIR EYES ARE TUBE SHAPED, AND THEY DO NOT MOVE.

50. AS IF THE PLATYPUS WASN'T WEIRD ENOUGH ALREADY, FEMALE PLATYPUSES FEED THEIR YOUNG BY "SWEATING" MILK THROUGH THEIR SKIN.

51. DADDY LONGLEGS HAVE BEEN AROUND SINCE BEFORE THE DINOSAURS.

52. AS ITS NAME IMPLIES, THE WEAVER ANT-MIMICKING JUMPING SPIDER LOOKS INCREDIBLY SIMILAR TO A WEAVER ANT.

However, a spider has eight legs, while an ant has only six. To account for this, the spider will often raise two of its legs to make them appear to be antennae. The spiders have been known to settle close to ant colonies and even pretend to be part of the colony!

53. ATLAS MOTHS CAN HAVE A WINGSPAN OF UP TO 10 INCHES (25 CENTIMETERS).

These silk-producing moths create incredibly large cocoons—so large that intact cocoons have been made into expensive change purses!

54. THE ELVIS PRESLEY SHIELD BUG IS A RARE GIANT SHIELD BUG WITH A UNIQUE SET OF MARKINGS.

Believe it or not, the black marks on its back have an uncanny resemblance to the eyes, nose, and hair of The King himself. (Other, less generous observers have likened its markings to Bert from *Sesame Street*.)

• 55 •

WHEN GARTER SNAKES MATE, THEY FORM A "MATING BALL" IN WHICH LARGE NUMBERS OF MALE SNAKES COMPETE TO MATE WITH A SINGLE FEMALE.

The mating ball is exactly what it sounds like: a writhing, slithering mass of snakes that looks like something out of a horror movie!

• 56 •

THE ASSASSIN BUG USES ITS SALIVA TO STICK THE CORPSES OF ITS VICTIMS ONTO A MOUND OF BODIES ON ITS BACK.

Scientists think this may be to make it appear bigger as a way of warding off predators, but whatever the reason, it's pretty grisly.

57. LEICHHARDT'S GRASSHOPPERS CAN LIVE ON A SINGLE PITYRODIA BUSH FOR THEIR ENTIRE LIVES.

The plant has an unpleasant, bitter flavor, and eating it makes the grasshoppers themselves less attractive to predators.

58. HERONS NEST IN THE SAME PLACE FOR MANY GENERATIONS.

This results in the creation of "heronries"—areas high up in the trees where dozens of nests are clustered together.

59. ALLIGATORS CAN HAVE UP TO 80 TEETH IN THEIR MOUTH AT ONCE.

They go through them quickly, though—the average alligator will lose around 3,000 teeth over the course of its life!

60. ZEBRAS CAN BE CROSSBRED WITH MANY OTHER EQUINES—AND THE NAMING CONVENTION FOR THEM IS PRETTY FUNNY.

Can you guess which equines were involved in creating the zorse, zebrule, zonkey, or zony?

61. PIGEONS ARE EXTREMELY INTELLIGENT.

Skills like counting are usually associated with primates, but the pigeon has demonstrated the ability to count to at least nine, which is comparable with most monkeys.

62. A MACAQUE ALMOST OWNED THE RIGHTS TO HIS PHOTOGRAPH.

In 2015, PETA sued a photographer on behalf of the macaque, who had taken a "selfie" using his camera. While the judge ultimately decided against PETA, it was the first time a court ruled on a case seeking to declare an animal the owner of property.

63. A GORILLA NAMED KOKO WAS A PIONEER FOR ANIMAL COMMUNICATION: SCIENTISTS WORKED TO TEACH KOKO AMERICAN SIGN LANGUAGE, AND BY THE TIME OF HER DEATH SHE COULD SIGN MORE THAN 1,000 WORDS.

64. A (FORMERLY) CAPTIVE EAGLE WENT ON THE RUN FROM THE POLICE FOR ALMOST TWO WEEKS.

After escaping the London Zoo, an eagle named Goldie evaded capture for 12 days, flying around the city and drawing crowds of onlookers wherever he went.

65. THE CANE TOAD'S LIBIDO IS...WELL, LET'S JUST SAY "UNRESTRAINED."

Cane toads have been observed attempting to mate with anything from mangoes to snakes.

66. EVERYONE KNOWS THAT OWLS CAN TURN THEIR HEADS ALMOST COMPLETELY AROUND, BUT DID YOU KNOW THAT OWLS HAVE "BACKUP ARTERIES" THAT TAKE OVER WHEN BLOOD VESSELS ARE CLOSED OFF BY THEIR HEAD SWIVELING?

• 67 •

HUMANS ARE APPARENTLY
NOT THE ONLY CREATURES
CAPABLE OF GOING TO WAR:
THE GOMBE CHIMPANZEE WAR
WAS A FOUR-YEAR CONFLICT
BETWEEN TWO RIVAL GROUPS
OF CHIMPANZEES THAT
ULTIMATELY RESULTED IN THE
ERADICATION OF ONE OF THEM.

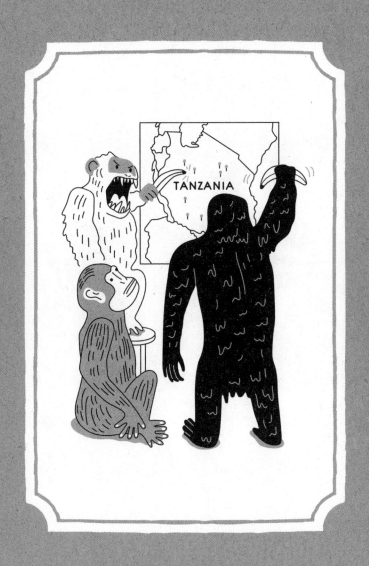

· 68 ·

THE SAN JOAQUIN KIT FOX HAS ADAPTED TO LIVE IN HUMAN-DOMINATED ENVIRONMENTS, EVOLVING TO FAVOR A DIET VERY SIMILAR TO HUMANS.

The result? Thanks to consuming corn syrup–heavy foods, the kit fox now has a problem with high cholesterol.

69. THE CHAMPAWAT TIGER WAS A FEMALE BENGAL TIGER THAT KILLED AN ESTIMATED 436 HUMANS IN THE LATE 1800S AND EARLY 1900S.

It is one of the most prolific hunters of humans in recorded history.

70. THE MOUNTAIN STONE WĒTĀ IS A LARGE INSECT NATIVE TO NEW ZEALAND THAT FREEZES COMPLETELY SOLID DURING THE WINTER—AND SURVIVES! AND BY THE WAY, THEY REALLY ARE "LARGE" INSECTS.

Don't look them up if you're afraid of bugs!

71. MICROSCOPIC (AND ADORABLE) TARDIGRADES ARE AMONG THE HARDIEST CREATURES ON EARTH.

They can survive some of the harshest environments imaginable, including the top of Mount Everest, the depths of the ocean, and even outer space.

72. THERE IS A SPECIES OF ARMADILLO KNOWN PRIMARILY FOR ITS HABIT OF "SCREAMING" WHEN HANDLED BY HUMANS.

Appropriately, it is known as the "screaming hairy armadillo."

73. THERE IS A SPECIES OF BEETLE WITH THE MAGICAL-SOUNDING SCIENTIFIC NAME OF *AGRA CADABRA*.

In fact, the genus *Agra* seems to lend itself to puns: it is also home to the *Agra vation* beetle.

74. IF YOU DON'T LIKE YOUR NAME, JUST REMEMBER THAT IT COULD ALWAYS BE WORSE: THERE IS A SPECIES OF BEETLE WITH THE UNFORTUNATE SCIENTIFIC NAME *COLON RECTUM*.

75. MARKHOR HORNS ARE UNIQUE IN THE ANIMAL KINGDOM: NOT ONLY DO THEY SPIRAL LIKE A CORKSCREW, BUT THEY CAN GROW MORE THAN 5 FEET LONG!

76. THE TARSIER, A PRIMATE NATIVE TO THE PHILIPPINES, HAS INCREDIBLY LARGE EYES FOR ITS SMALL BODY.

If humans had eyes with the same proportion to our bodies, they would be the size of grapefruits!

77. NAKED MOLE RATS ARE NOTABLE FOR THEIR EXTREME RESISTANCE TO CANCER.

Scientists studying them think they may hold the key to eradicating cancer for good.

78. AN AVERAGE MOLE EATS BETWEEN 40 POUNDS AND 50 POUNDS (BETWEEN 18 KILOGRAMS AND 23 KILOGRAMS) OF EARTHWORMS EVERY YEAR!

• 79 •

DESPITE ITS RELATIVELY SMALL SIZE, THE GIANT ANTEATER HAS THE LONGEST TONGUE OF ANY LAND MAMMAL.

The anteater's tongue can be up to 24 inches (61 centimeters) long, dwarfing the tongues of much larger creatures.

· 80 ·

THE WOLVERINE FROG PRODUCES "CLAWS" BY BREAKING ITS OWN BONES AND PUSHING THEM THROUGH ITS SKIN.

It's easy to see where it gets its name—the Wolverine frog even has hairlike "sideburns" that give it a striking resemblance to the famous comic book character.

81. TRUE OR FALSE: SNAILS CAN SLEEP FOR UP TO THREE YEARS.

False. This myth is surprisingly common! Snails can hibernate for a prolonged period of time, but hibernation and sleep are not the same. And while hibernation has been observed to last upward of three years, those cases are extremely rare.

82. TRUE OR FALSE: THE FIRST LIVING CREATURE TO BE INTENTIONALLY SENT INTO SPACE WAS A DOG.

False. Surprisingly, the first living creatures to be sent into space were fruit flies launched by the United States, aboard captured German rockets.

83. TRUE OR FALSE: THE MOSQUITO KILLS MORE HUMANS THAN ANY OTHER ANIMAL ON EARTH.

True. Thanks to their ability to spread bloodborne diseases like malaria, mosquitoes are responsible for between 725,000 and 1,000,000 human deaths per year.

84. TRUE OR FALSE: TURKEYS HAVE BEEN KNOWN TO DROWN DURING RAINSTORMS BECAUSE THEY LOOK STRAIGHT UP AT THE SKY.

False. This myth has persisted for many years, but it has no basis in fact. Turkeys may not be the smartest animals, but if they were that dumb, they'd never survive at all!

85. TRUE OR FALSE: HORSES DREAM, BUT ONLY WHEN THEY ARE LYING DOWN.

True. Horses can sleep standing up or lying down, but they are only capable of achieving REM sleep when they are lying on the ground.

86. TRUE OR FALSE: MOSQUITOES HAVE A PREFERENCE FOR CERTAIN BLOOD TYPES.

True. Researchers have found that mosquitoes are more attracted to people with type O blood than any other blood type.

87. TRUE OR FALSE: DESPITE THEIR INCREDIBLE SIZE, HIPPOS ARE VERY FAST.

True. An adult hippopotamus can run about 19 mph (31 kmh). The average human running speed is only around 6 mph (10 kmh).

88. TRUE OR FALSE: BARN OWLS MATE FOR LIFE.

True. But it's not the most interesting fact about barn owl partnerships; despite mating for life, about 25% of couples eventually separate.

89. TRUE OR FALSE: OSTRICHES WILL SOMETIMES BURY THEIR HEADS IN THE SAND TO "HIDE" FROM PREDATORS.

False. Despite the popularity of this "fact," it is not true. Ostriches do sometimes stick their heads in the ground, but only to adjust the eggs in their sandy nests.

• 90 •

TRUE OR FALSE: IT IS ILLEGAL TO OPEN AN UMBRELLA NEAR A HORSE IN NEW YORK.

True. The law feels strange and outdated today, but it made sense at the time it was passed: when horses were everywhere, spooking one with an umbrella could spell disaster.

· 91 ·

TRUE OR FALSE: A BEAR FOUGHT FOR THE NAZIS IN WORLD WAR II.

False. Just the opposite, in fact! A bear named Wojtek was "enlisted" in the Polish army, and was used to carry artillery and generally raise the morale of the soldiers. Wojtek was very friendly, having been raised by humans since he was a cub.

92. TRUE OR FALSE: THERE IS A SPECIES OF SPIDER KNOWN AS THE SPARKLEMUFFIN.

True. Sparklemuffin is the colloquial name for the *Maratus jactatus* jumping spider, native to Australia.

93. TRUE OR FALSE: KOALAS HAVE FINGERPRINTS THAT ARE ALMOST INDISTINGUISHABLE FROM HUMAN FINGERPRINTS.

True. Just don't expect "A koala did it!" to hold up in court.

94. TRUE OR FALSE: A PELICAN'S STOMACH CAN HOLD THREE TIMES AS MUCH WATER AS THE POUCH ON ITS BILL.

False. Actually, the pelican can hold three gallons (11 liters) of water in its pouch, compared to just one gallon (four liters) in its stomach.

95. TRUE OR FALSE: NOT ALL ANIMALS HAVE BRAINS.

True. There are quite a few examples of animals without a brain, including the sea urchin and earthworm.

96. TRUE OR FALSE: BEAVERS HAVE METAL TEETH.

True. Strange though it may sound, beavers have iron in their tooth enamel, rather than the magnesium typical of other rodents. This gives their teeth a slightly orange color and makes them harder.

97. TRUE OR FALSE: A SMALL SWARM OF LOCUSTS CONSUMES ROUGHLY THE SAME AMOUNT OF FOOD AS A FAMILY OF FIVE.

False. Not even close. In fact, a small swarm of locusts can consume the same amount of food as 35,000 people.

98. TRUE OR FALSE: THE ALPINE SWIFT CAN STAY IN THE AIR FOR SIX MONTHS WITHOUT LANDING.

True. Amazingly, scientists have observed these birds flying for 200 days straight.

99. TRUE OR FALSE: NAPOLEON BONAPARTE, EMPEROR OF FRANCE, WAS ONCE ATTACKED BY A SWARM OF RABBITS.

True. Napoleon's men set loose more than 3,000 domesticated rabbits. Thinking it was feeding time, the rabbits swarmed Napoleon and his party. Unable to position his gun to shoot them, Napoleon ultimately fled to his palace.

· 100 ·

TRUE OR FALSE: THE HORNED DUNG BEETLE CAN PULL MORE THAN 1,000 TIMES ITS OWN BODY WEIGHT.

True. It's one of nature's strongest creatures, capable of pulling an estimated 1,141 times its body weight.

{ Plants & Fungi }

Yes, yes. Plants and fungi are not the same thing. That's not an unbelievable fact—it's a fact everyone already knows. But for the sake of simplicity, let's consider them together—a fact salad, if you will, with facts about mushrooms enhancing facts about lettuce and kale. Did you know, for example, that there is a mushroom with its own self-destruct mechanism? Or that banana "trees" are technically herbs? Don't make the mistake of believing plants and fungi are boring just because they don't move around like animals—they can be deeply fascinating too.

1. THE OLDEST TREE IN THE WORLD IS BELIEVED TO BE ROUGHLY 5,000 YEARS OLD.

2. IN 1971, ASTRONAUTS BROUGHT SEEDS TO THE MOON, WHICH WERE LATER PLANTED BACK ON EARTH.

3. SCIENTISTS ESTIMATE THAT IT TAKES BETWEEN 225 AND 734 TREES TO OFFSET THE CARBON DIOXIDE EMISSIONS OF ONE CAR.

4. THERE ARE APPROXIMATELY 73,000 DIFFERENT SPECIES OF TREES ON THE PLANET EARTH.

5. WHILE IT CAN VARY GREATLY BASED ON THE SIZE OF THE TREE, OVER 8,000 SHEETS OF PAPER CAN BE MANUFACTURED FROM THE AVERAGE TREE.

6. BAMBOO IS ONE OF THE FASTEST-GROWING PLANTS ON EARTH, AND CAN GROW UPWARD OF 35 INCHES (89 CENTIMETERS) IN A SINGLE DAY.

7. THE SWEET, YELLOW BANANAS WE KNOW TODAY ARE A RELATIVELY RECENT MUTATION, FIRST DISCOVERED IN 1836.

Before that, bananas were green or red in color and typically only used in cooking.

8. IT IS COMMONLY KNOWN THAT THE TOMATO IS TECHNICALLY A FRUIT, NOT A VEGETABLE.

However, in 1893, the US Supreme Court ruled that the tomato should be considered a vegetable for the purposes of tariffs, imports, and customs.

9. A FIG TREE IN SOUTH AFRICA WAS FOUND TO HAVE ROOTS REACHING MORE THAN 400 FEET (122 METERS) DEEP.

Considering that the average fig tree only requires approximately 5 feet (1.5 meters) of soil, that's quite an accomplishment!

10. NIGER'S TREE OF TÉNÉRÉ WAS KNOWN AS THE "MOST ISOLATED TREE IN THE WORLD."

Despite being the only tree for 250 miles, it was felled by a drunk driver in 1973.

11. CERTAIN FRUITS, SUCH AS NAVEL ORANGES, ARE GENETIC MUTATIONS THAT CANNOT REPRODUCE NATURALLY.

As a result, every navel orange is a clone!

12. A SINGLE YUBARI MELON GENERALLY COSTS BETWEEN $50 AND $100, BUT IN 2019 A PAIR OF PARTICULARLY HIGH-GRADE MELONS SOLD FOR ROUGHLY $45,000 AT AUCTION.

Get your melon baller out!

• 13 •

FOLLOWING A RAINSTORM, SOME CHERRY FARMERS HIRE HELICOPTER PILOTS TO "BLOW-DRY" THEIR TREES TO PREVENT THE CHERRIES FROM SPLITTING OPEN DUE TO EXCESSIVE MOISTURE.

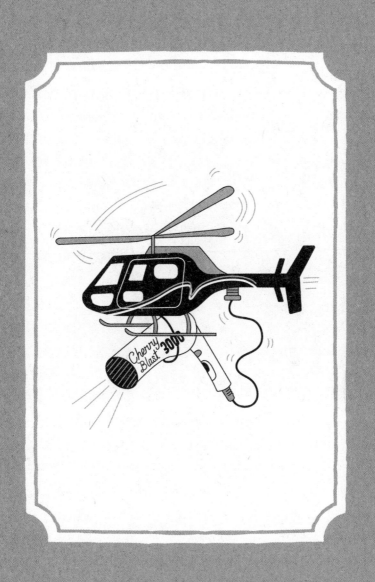

• 14 •

CASHEWS ARE
TECHNICALLY SEEDS, NOT
NUTS, AND THEY SPROUT
FROM THE BOTTOM OF
THE "CASHEW APPLE."

15. FOR MORE THAN 70 YEARS, THE UNITED STATES HAD A "NATIONAL RAISIN RESERVE" THAT FARMERS WERE REQUIRED BY LAW TO CONTRIBUTE TO.

Originally dating back to the Great Depression, the National Raisin Reserve was finally shut down in 2015, after the US Supreme Court ruled it violated private property protections.

16. USING A TECHNIQUE KNOWN AS GRAFTING, FARMERS CAN CREATE TREES CAPABLE OF BEARING MULTIPLE DIFFERENT TYPES OF FRUIT.

17. ONLY ABOUT 5% OF US CRANBERRIES ARE SOLD FRESH.

The remaining 95% are turned into cranberry juice, cranberry sauce, and other products.

18. CERTAIN PINE TREES HAVE EVOLVED TO NOT JUST SURVIVE FOREST FIRES, BUT TO THRIVE IN THEIR AFTERMATH.

19. THE JUG-SHAPED PITCHER PLANT HAS EVOLVED A RATHER UNUSUAL SYMBIOTIC RELATIONSHIP WITH THE TREE SHREW: THE TREE SHREW USES THE PITCHER PLANT AS A TOILET, AND THE PITCHER PLANT CONSUMES THE VALUABLE NITROGEN IN ITS WASTE.

20. DINNERPLATE DAHLIAS PRODUCE HUGE BLOSSOMS THAT CAN REACH DIAMETERS OF 10 INCHES (25 CENTIMETERS) ACROSS.

21. GARLIC HAS ANTIBIOTIC AND ANTIFUNGAL PROPERTIES THAT MAKE IT AN EFFECTIVE ACNE TREATMENT.

Simply mince some garlic and rub it on a pimple!

22. ECHINACEA, KNOWN FOR ITS SPINY SEED CONE, IS ONE OF THE MOST WIDELY USED HERBS FOR MEDICINAL PURPOSES.

Lab studies have shown that it can boost immune function.

23. PERHAPS THE MOST UNSETTLING THING ABOUT THE FAMOUS CORPSE FLOWER ISN'T ITS LEGENDARY STINK, BUT ITS TEMPERATURE.

Unlike most plants, the corpse flower is warm—in fact, it can reach 98 degrees Fahrenheit (36.7 degrees Celsius), approximately the same temperature as the human body. Creepy!

24. TREES CAN CONNECT TO—AND EVEN COMMUNICATE WITH—ONE ANOTHER VIA UNDERGROUND NETWORKS OF TINY, HAIRLIKE FUNGAL FILAMENTS CALLED MYCORRHIZAL NETWORKS.

German forester Peter Wohlleben calls it the "woodwide web."

• 25 •

DAHLIAS, STUNNING
FLOWERS POPULAR IN
WEDDING ARRANGEMENTS
AND SUMMER GARDENS,
WERE ORIGINALLY
CLASSIFIED AS VEGETABLES
BECAUSE THEIR EDIBLE
TUBERS TASTE LIKE A
POTATO-RADISH HYBRID.

• 26 •

IN THE 1600S, TULIPS WERE SO POPULAR THAT A SINGLE BULB COULD COST MORE THAN A HOUSE.

In fact, tulip bulbs were even used as currency in some cases. This "tulip mania" briefly crashed the entire Dutch economy!

27. MUSHROOMS ARE A REMARKABLY SUSTAINABLE CROP: THEY DON'T REQUIRE LIGHT TO GROW, AND A SINGLE ACRE OF GROWING SPACE CAN PRODUCE UP TO ONE MILLION POUNDS OF MUSHROOMS PER YEAR.

28. BELIEVE IT OR NOT, ALL TEA COMES FROM THE *CAMELLIA SINENSIS* PLANT.

The differences between black tea, green tea, oolong tea, and all other teas have nothing to do with the tea leaves themselves, and everything to do with how they are processed.

29. BEFORE TREES EVOLVED ON EARTH, THE LANDSCAPE WAS COVERED IN GIGANTIC MUSHROOMS THAT COULD GROW TO 26 FEET (8 METERS) TALL AND 3 FEET (ONE METER) WIDE.

They didn't look like today's mushrooms, though—instead, they were mostly just one tall stalk.

30. MUSHROOMS HAVE AN EXCEPTIONALLY FAST GROWTH RATE AND CAN DOUBLE IN SIZE WITHIN 24 HOURS.

31. BANANA "TREES" ARE TECHNICALLY HERBS—DISTANTLY RELATED TO GINGER!

When most people think of herbs, they think of things like rosemary or basil. But more fibrous and woody herbs like ginger and horseradish are not uncommon.

32. IN 2012, SCIENTISTS WERE ABLE TO GROW A PLANT THAT HAD BEEN EXTINCT FOR OVER 30,000 YEARS, USING ANCIENT SEEDS PRESERVED IN THE SIBERIAN PERMAFROST.

33. THERE ARE APPROXIMATELY 1,500–1,800 SPECIES OF CACTI—AND ONLY ONE OF THEM ORIGINATES OUTSIDE OF THE AMERICAS. THE MISTLETOE CACTUS COMES FROM AFRICA AND ASIA, AND SCIENTISTS SPECULATE THAT IT MAY HAVE BEEN TRANSPLANTED FROM THE AMERICAS BY MIGRATORY BIRDS SOMETIME IN THE DISTANT PAST.

34. SCIENTISTS ESTIMATE THAT AS MANY AS 40% OF THE PLANTS AND FUNGI ON THE PLANET ARE AT RISK OF EXTINCTION TODAY, WITH CLIMATE CHANGE AND DEFORESTATION LISTED AS THE PRIMARY CULPRITS.

35. THE WORLD'S LARGEST SEED IS THE COCO DE MER (ALSO CALLED THE SEA COCONUT OR DOUBLE COCONUT), WHICH CAN GROW TO 12 INCHES (30 CENTIMETERS) LONG AND WEIGH OVER 40 POUNDS (18 KILOGRAMS)!

36. SCIENTISTS ESTIMATE THAT THERE COULD BE AS MANY AS FIVE MILLION TO 50 MILLION SPECIES OF PLANTS ON EARTH.

Amazingly, we have discovered fewer than two million so far—which means that we have quite a few to find!

• 37 •

THERE IS A PLANT IN SOUTH AFRICA KNOWN AS THE "BASEBALL PLANT."

As you might expect, its size and appearance mimic that of a baseball almost perfectly!

· 38 ·

CERTAIN MUSHROOMS CAN DIGEST PLASTIC.

This isn't just cool—it might play a major role in helping to fight pollution.

39. EATING A RIPE BANANA CAN BE USED TO TREAT CONSTIPATION.

However, eating an unripe banana can actually cause constipation!

40. MUSHROOMS ARE THE FRUITING BODY OF THE FUNGUS.

They're basically the fungus equivalent of an apple or an orange!

41. LIGHTNING STRIKES MAKE MUSHROOMS MULTIPLY AT A MUCH FASTER RATE—AND SCIENTISTS AREN'T SURE WHY.

42. THE SHAGGY INK CAP MUSHROOM HAS A SELF-DESTRUCT MECHANISM.

Once the mushroom is picked, it releases a black goo that causes the mushroom to digest itself within 24 hours. They're delicious, but you'd better cook them quickly!

43. THE BUTTON, CREMINI, AND PORTOBELLO MUSHROOMS YOU SEE IN THE STORE ARE ALL THE SAME TYPE OF MUSHROOM—JUST AT DIFFERENT STAGES OF THE LIFE CYCLE.

44. IN ANCIENT EGYPT, MUSHROOMS WERE SO REVERED THAT COMMONERS WERE NOT ALLOWED TO TOUCH THEM AND ONLY ROYALS WERE ALLOWED TO EAT THEM.

45. SILPHIUM WAS A NATURALLY CONTRACEPTIVE HERB POPULAR IN THE ROMAN EMPIRE.

It was so popular, in fact, that the Romans drove it to extinction due to overcultivation.

46. THE LARGEST ORGANISM ON EARTH IS A FUNGUS! THE HONEY MUSHROOM IS BELIEVED TO BE OVER 8,000 YEARS OLD AND COVERS ROUGHLY 2.5 SQUARE MILES (6.5 SQUARE KILOMETERS) OF OREGON'S MALHEUR NATIONAL FOREST.

47. THANKS TO THE VIDEO GAME (AND HBO SHOW) *THE LAST OF US*, MOST PEOPLE ARE NOW AWARE OF THE *CORDYCEPS* FUNGUS THAT CAN HIJACK THE BRAIN OF AN ANT.

However, there are other fungi that form a more cooperative relationship with ants. In exchange for a regular supply of small mushrooms to consume, ants in South America provide the *Leucoagaricus gongylophorus* fungus with a steady supply of leaves to eat—sometimes up to 50,000 leaves a day!

48. SPEAKING OF *CORDYCEPS*: A TYPE OF *CORDYCEPS* FUNGUS THAT GROWS FROM THE BODY OF A CATERPILLAR IS ONE OF THE MOST EXPENSIVE FOODS IN THE WORLD.

Just one pound (about half a kilogram) has been known to sell for as much as $63,000!

• 49 •

THE "CROOKED FOREST" IN POLAND HAS MORE THAN 400 TREES THAT SHARE A STRANGE FEATURE: THEY ARE COILED AT THE BASE, GIVING THEM A SNAKELIKE APPEARANCE.

Stranger still, no one seems to know the cause of this malformation.

· 50 ·

WHITE BANEBERRY PLANTS ARE OFTEN REFERRED TO AS "DOLL'S EYES," BECAUSE— YOU GUESSED IT—THEIR BERRIES LOOK EERILY LIKE TINY EYEBALLS.

It's probably good that they are so creepy looking, because the berries are also highly poisonous.

51. THERE IS A WEED IN THE UNITED STATES, KNOWN AS THE "GIANT COW PARSNIP," THAT IS SO NOXIOUS IT CAN CAUSE SEVERE BURNS AND BLISTERS JUST BY TOUCHING IT.

52. FRANCE'S KING HENRY IV WAS BAPTIZED IN WATER CONTAINING GARLIC.

This was because garlic was believed to help ward off both diseases and evil spirits.

53. DEADLY NIGHTSHADE IS, AS ITS NAME IMPLIES, ONE OF THE MOST POISONOUS PLANTS IN THE WORLD.

However, it also causes the pupils to dilate, a feature that once led to its use as a beauty product. Putting deadly nightshade in your eyes is not recommended today, as absorbing too much of it can cause blindness—and even death.

54. THE MANCHINEEL TREE MIGHT JUST BE THE MOST DANGEROUS TREE IN THE WORLD: NOT ONLY IS ITS FRUIT HIGHLY POISONOUS (CAPABLE OF KILLING A GROWN HUMAN WITH A SINGLE BITE), BUT ITS BARK AND SAP ARE ALSO HIGHLY POISONOUS AND ACIDIC.

Even its leaves pose a significant danger: if burned, the smoke they give off can cause blindness. If you're ever in the Caribbean or Central American regions, maybe just give this tree a wide berth.

55. **MANY BIBLICAL SCHOLARS BELIEVE THAT THE "CROWN OF THORNS" PLACED ON CHRIST'S HEAD DURING THE CRUCIFIXION WAS A PLANT KNOWN AS *EUPHORBIA MILII*.**

Appropriately, the plant is often referred to as the "Christ plant" or the "crown of thorns" and is a surprisingly common houseplant today.

56. **THE BLEEDING TOOTH FUNGUS MIGHT BE THE MOST HORRIBLE-LOOKING (AND HORRIBLY NAMED) FUNGUS IN THE WORLD.**

Amazingly, it isn't toxic—though you probably wouldn't want to eat it, due to its bitter taste. And, you know, the fact that it looks like something out of a horror movie.

57. **STUDIES HAVE PRODUCED EVIDENCE THAT, DESPITE NOT HAVING A BRAIN, THE PEA PLANT CAN MAKE "DECISIONS" BASED ON A RUDIMENTARY FORM OF RISK ANALYSIS.**

58. **THERE IS AN ASPEN FOREST IN UTAH THAT IS TECHNICALLY ONE GIANT ORGANISM. DUBBED "PANDO," IT IS MADE UP OF MORE THAN 47,000 TRUNKS THAT ALL SHARE ONE ROOT SYSTEM.**

59. **KALE, BROCCOLI, CAULIFLOWER, CABBAGE, AND BRUSSELS SPROUTS ALL COME FROM THE SAME PLANT SPECIES.**

They are different today because farmers selectively bred them for certain edible features.

· 60 ·

THE *PSEUDOCOLUS FUSIFORMIS* FUNGUS IS KNOWN AS THE "STINKY SQUID" BECAUSE IT LOOKS LIKE SQUID TENTACLES EMERGING FROM THE GROUND AND, WELL, IT SMELLS QUITE BAD.

· 61 ·

EVERYONE KNOWS THAT PLANTS LIKE THE VENUS FLYTRAP EAT BUGS.

But did you know that some carnivorous plants are large enough to consume reptiles, and even small mammals?

62. TREES ARE ALMOST ENTIRELY MADE UP OF DEAD CELLS.

Only about 1% of a tree is made up of cells that are biologically alive.

63. TOMATO PLANTS ARE HERMAPHRODITIC: THEIR FLOWERS CONTAIN BOTH MALE AND FEMALE REPRODUCTIVE ORGANS, AND THEY CAN (AND DO!) SELF-FERTILIZE.

64. DESPITE BEING KNOWN FOR ITS ROMANTIC ASSOCIATION, MISTLETOE IS ACTUALLY POISONOUS.

65. THE GYMPIE-GYMPIE PLANT CONTAINS STINGING NETTLES THAT CAUSE PAIN SO SEVERE THAT IT HAS BEEN KNOWN TO DRIVE HUMANS TO SUICIDE.

The plant is colloquially known as the "suicide plant."

66. THERE IS A FLOWER CALLED THE "NAKED MAN ORCHID," AND, AS YOU MIGHT EXPECT, ITS FLOWERS LOOK ALMOST EXACTLY LIKE A NAKED MAN WEARING A HAT.

67. WITCH'S HAIR (ALSO KNOWN AS STRANGLE WEED) IS A STRANGE-LOOKING PLANT WITH A TWISTED, SPAGHETTILIKE APPEARANCE.

It has no chlorophyll, and instead feeds off other plants.

68. AFRICAN BAOBAB TREES DON'T GROW TREE RINGS LIKE MOST OTHER TREES, MAKING IT DIFFICULT TO KNOW HOW OLD THEY ARE.

Some years, they grow no rings at all. Other years, they grow multiple rings.

69. THE *HYDNORA* PLANT IS ONE OF THE MOST TERRIFYING-LOOKING PLANTS ON EARTH, WITH AN APPEARANCE LIKE A VERTICAL, TOOTH-LINED MOUTH.

Appropriately, it is a parasitic plant that draw its nutrients from the root systems of other plants.

70. THE "DANCING PLANT" IS A PLANT THAT MOVES AND VIBRATES IN RESPONSE TO STIMULI LIKE SUNLIGHT OR SOUND.

It gets its name because it appears to respond to music!

71. THE SANDBOX TREE IS EXTREMELY DANGEROUS: NOT ONLY IS THE TREE ITSELF COVERED IN SMALL SPIKES, BUT ITS FRUIT EXPLODES WHEN RIPE, SENDING SEEDS FLYING AT SPEEDS OF 150 MPH (241 KMH).

It is often referred to as the "dynamite tree."

72. ACCORDING TO THEIR WEBSITE, THE POISON GARDEN AT THE ALNWICK GARDEN IN THE UK IS FILLED EXCLUSIVELY WITH 100 "TOXIC, INTOXICATING, AND NARCOTIC PLANTS."

Yikes!

• 73 •

THE *MIMOSA PUDICA* PLANT
IS SOMETIMES REFERRED TO
AS THE "VIRGIN TREE" OR
"SHAME TREE" BECAUSE ITS
LEAVES FOLD UP TO SHIELD
THEMSELVES IN RESPONSE
TO BEING TOUCHED.

74. MOSS IS SOMETIMES USED AS AN ENVIRONMENTALLY FRIENDLY FORM OF "ECO-GRAFFITI."

Because moss grows easily, has no roots, and requires little upkeep, it is easy for demonstrators to use for writing messages on walls and other surfaces.

75. MARIGOLDS HAVE A LONG HISTORY OF VARIED USES: ANCIENT RECORDS INDICATE THAT THE AZTECS MAY HAVE USED THEM TO TREAT PEOPLE WHO HAD BEEN STRUCK BY LIGHTNING...

and as a cure for hiccups.

76. THE OLDEST KNOWN FLOWER SPECIES IS THE *MONTSECHIA*.

We have found intact fossils that date back 130 million years!

77. RECENT STUDIES HAVE SHOWN THAT PLANTS EMIT SOUNDS WHEN THEY ARE "STRESSED."

The sounds are inaudible to humans but can be measured with sensitive equipment.

78. THE OLEANDER IS THE OFFICIAL FLOWER OF HIROSHIMA, BECAUSE IT WAS THE FIRST FLOWER TO BLOOM WITHIN THE RUBBLE AFTER THE DROPPING OF THE ATOMIC BOMB.

79. THE FLAVOR OF BRUSSELS SPROUTS HAS CHANGED CONSIDERABLY OVER TIME.

Today's brussels sprouts taste significantly less bitter than they did before the 1990s. Thanks to some creative breeding, brussels sprouts have enjoyed a resurgence in popularity.

80. IN ANCIENT ROME, BASIL WAS A SYMBOL OF HATRED.

It was believed to only grow where there was hatred and abuse.

81. TRUE OR FALSE: LEMONS ARE NOT A NATURALLY OCCURRING FRUIT, BUT A MAN-MADE CREATION.

False. A surprising number of people believe this myth, but lemons are, in fact, a natural hybrid of oranges and citrons.

82. TRUE OR FALSE: EATING PINEAPPLE DISSOLVES THE FLESH IN YOUR MOUTH.

True. Granted, it happens on a very small scale—but this is why pineapple can sting the inside of your mouth. Pineapples contain an enzyme that breaks down meat (which is why BBQ experts will tell you to be very careful about using pineapple juice).

83. TRUE OR FALSE: THE "JUMPING CACTUS" GETS ITS NAME BECAUSE OF ITS TENDENCY TO FALL ON TOP OF PASSERSBY.

False. The jumping cactus doesn't actually jump, but its pieces detach extremely easily, often latching onto clothing or flesh at the slightest touch.

• 84 •

TRUE OR FALSE: PLANTS SLEEP.

True. Well, mostly true, at least. They don't "sleep" in the same way animals do, because plants are not conscious. But they have a natural circadian rhythm, just like us, with more and less active periods.

· 85 ·

TRUE OR FALSE: SOME WATER LILIES CAN GROW LARGE ENOUGH FOR A GROWN PERSON TO STAND ON.

True. You would have to be a small person, but still: the giant Victoria water lily can grow to 10 feet (3 meters) wide and hold nearly 100 pounds (45 kilograms)! Some exceptionally large specimens have even been reported to hold more than 400 pounds (181 kilograms).

86. TRUE OR FALSE: CACTI REALLY DO CONTAIN WATER.

True. It's not the most appetizing water—it tends to be thicker and stickier than the regular stuff—but it can save your life in a pinch.

87. TRUE OR FALSE: FLOWERS CAN SENSE BEES BUZZING NEARBY.

True. Flowers can "hear" the buzzing of bees. Evidence suggests they attempt to lure them closer by increasing their sugar content.

88. TRUE OR FALSE: SOME OF WHAT WE THINK OF AS FRUITS AND VEGETABLES ARE ACTUALLY FLOWERS, INCLUDING ARTICHOKES, BROCCOLI, AND CAULIFLOWERS.

True. You'd be surprised how many flowers you probably eat on a regular basis!

89. TRUE OR FALSE: BABY CARROTS ARE GENETICALLY MODIFIED, TINY CARROTS.

False. What we know as "baby carrots" are actually full-size carrots carved down to a tiny size. They are basically all marketing!

90. TRUE OR FALSE: HOLLYHOCK FLOWERS WERE ONCE KNOWN AS "OUTHOUSE FLOWERS" BECAUSE OF THEIR UNPLEASANT ODOR.

False. They were indeed called outhouse flowers, but that's only because people planted them around outhouses. The reason was simple: hollyhocks grow tall enough to obscure the unsightly outhouses from view.

91. TRUE OR FALSE: SCIENTISTS CAN ACCURATELY DATE VOLCANIC ERUPTIONS BASED ON THE IMPACT THEY HAVE ON TREE RINGS.

True. The dust kicked up by eruptions has a visible effect on tree ring formation.

92. TRUE OR FALSE: SOME PLANTS CAN COUNT.

True. The Venus flytrap, for example, only closes after it has been touched a certain number of times. Scientists believe that some plants can "count" to at least five!

93. TRUE OR FALSE: DANDELIONS ARE POISONOUS TO HUMANS.

False. Not only are dandelions edible, but they also contain significant amounts of both vitamin A and vitamin C and were once used to prevent and treat scurvy!

• 94 •

TRUE OR FALSE: A FARMER ONCE MANAGED TO CREATE A HYBRID BETWEEN CORN AND TOBACCO.

False. In reality, the farmer created a hybrid between tomatoes and tobacco. The so-called "tomacco" was inspired by a *Simpsons* episode and bore fruit for 18 months.

95. TRUE OR FALSE: CERTAIN PLANT BULBS CAN ACTUALLY PULL THEMSELVES DEEPER INTO THE GROUND IF THEY ARE PLANTED TOO SHALLOW.

True. Tulips are one example of a plant that can do this.

96. TRUE OR FALSE: THERE ARE TECHNICALLY ONLY SEVEN VARIETIES OF POTATOES.

False. In fact, there are close to 4,000 varieties of potatoes! They were first documented as far back as 8000 BC.

97. TRUE OR FALSE: FAR FROM KILLING WHEAT CROPS, SNOW CAN ACTUALLY BE GOOD FOR WHEAT.

True. Snow can provide a layer of insulation that protects wheat crops from fluctuating winter temperatures. When it melts, it can also provide valuable moisture for the soil.

98. TRUE OR FALSE: CARING FOR HOUSEPLANTS HAS BEEN SHOWN TO MAKE HUMANS MORE STRESSED.

False. Just the opposite, in fact. Studies have shown that indoor plants reduce stress and increase happiness levels.

99. TRUE OR FALSE: PLANTS CAN BE ALBINO, JUST LIKE ANIMALS.

True. However, albino plants lack the chlorophyll they need to make food, and, as a result, they rarely survive long.

100. TRUE OR FALSE: IN ANCIENT ROME, BEETS WERE CONSIDERED AN APHRODISIAC.

True. It seems strange now, but the Romans really did sip beet juice to get in the mood.

[**The Watery World**]

A wise woman once said, "Don't go chasing waterfalls/Please stick to the rivers and the lakes that you're used to." But that's silly—after all, if you stick to familiar waters, how will you ever learn about manatees and their armpit nipples? Or creepy fish with human teeth? A lot of weird and wonderful creatures call our oceans home—as well as some spooky ones that might just inspire you to stick to dry land.

1. **WHEN A DOLPHIN SLEEPS, ONLY HALF OF ITS BRAIN RESTS AT A TIME.**

   This allows it to rest without fully losing consciousness.

2. **DOLPHINS HAVE BEEN OBSERVED INGESTING PUFFER FISH NERVE TOXINS AND PASSING THEM AROUND IN AN APPARENT EFFORT TO GET HIGH.**

3. **WHEN A PISTOL SHRIMP (OR "SNAPPING SHRIMP") SNAPS ITS CLAW, IT CREATES A JET OF WATER THAT CAN REACH 60 MPH (97 KMH) AND INSTANTLY STUN ITS PREY.**

4. **SCALLOPS HAVE UP TO 200 TINY EYES LINING THE OUTER EDGE OF THEIR BODIES.**

5. **WHEN A BLUE WHALE POOPS, IT CAN EVACUATE MORE THAN 50 GALLONS (189 LITERS) OF WASTE AT ONCE.**

6. **CLOWN FISH CAN CHANGE THEIR GENDER! ALL CLOWN FISH BEGIN LIFE AS MALES, BUT EVENTUALLY BECOME FEMALES AS THEY GROW OLDER.**

7. **THE BOWHEAD WHALE CAN LIVE TO APPROXIMATELY 200 YEARS OLD, GIVING IT THE LONGEST LIFE SPAN OF ANY KNOWN MAMMAL.**

8. AN OCTOPUS HAS NINE BRAINS: A CENTRAL BRAIN IN ITS HEAD, AND A SMALLER BRAIN IN EACH OF ITS ARMS.

9. SCALLOPED HAMMERHEAD SHARKS STAY WARM WHILE PLUNGING INTO THE EXTREME COLD OF DEEP WATERS TO HUNT BY HOLDING THEIR BREATH IN A UNIQUE WAY: CLOSING THEIR GILLS.

10. DEMON CATSHARKS ARE SO NAMED BECAUSE OF THEIR SPOOKY, BRIGHT-WHITE IRISES, WHICH IS A RARE PHYSICAL TRAIT FOR DEEPWATER SHARKS.

11. SEAHORSES ARE ONE OF ONLY A HANDFUL OF SPECIES ON EARTH WHERE THE MALE BECOMES PREGNANT AND GIVES BIRTH RATHER THAN THE FEMALE.

12. SURPRISINGLY, THE ANIMAL WITH THE LARGEST PENIS RELATIVE TO ITS SIZE IS THE BARNACLE! THE BARNACLE'S REPRODUCTIVE ORGAN CAN BE UP TO EIGHT TIMES LARGER THAN ITS BODY.

13. HUMAN BEINGS HAVE ONLY MAPPED BETWEEN 5% AND 10% OF THE EARTH'S OCEANS.

That's a lot of exploring left to do!

• 14 •

THE OCTOPUS IS ONE OF THE SMARTEST CREATURES ON EARTH. IN FACT, THOSE IN CAPTIVITY HAVE BEEN OBSERVED OPENING THEIR TANKS, CATCHING AND EATING FISH FROM NEIGHBORING TANKS, AND RETURNING TO THEIR OWN TANKS.

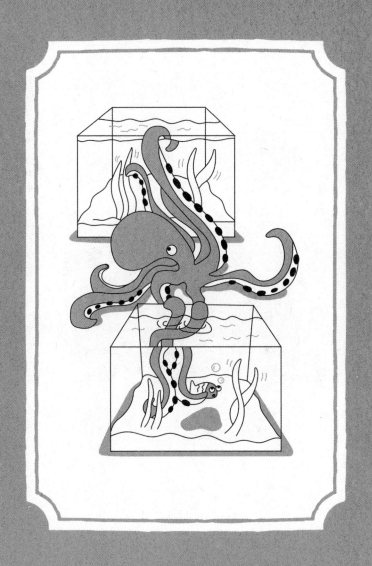

· 15 ·

WHEN PUFFER FISH
MATE, THEY LEAVE
BEHIND STRANGE (AND
BEAUTIFUL) UNDERWATER
"CROP CIRCLES."

16. WATERMEAL (ALSO KNOWN AS "DUCKWEED") IS THE SMALLEST FLOWERING PLANT ON EARTH.

It's barely larger than a grain of sand—in fact, the plant gets its name from the fact that it looks like green cornmeal floating on the surface of the water!

17. THE LARGEST TSUNAMI EVER RECORDED WAS OVER 1,700 FEET (518 METERS) TALL AND STRUCK ALASKA'S LITUYA BAY IN 1958.

Amazingly, of the six people in the bay at the time, four survived.

18. SCIENTISTS AND HISTORIANS ESTIMATE THAT THERE ARE OVER THREE MILLION SHIPWRECKS LITTERING THE OCEAN FLOOR—AND ONLY AROUND 1% OF THEM HAVE BEEN DOCUMENTED AND EXPLORED.

19. THE MARIANA TRENCH IS DEEPER THAN MOUNT EVEREST IS TALL.

While Mount Everest is 5.5 miles (8.9 kilometers) tall at its peak, the Mariana Trench reaches a depth of 6.8 miles (11 kilometers).

20. EGYPTIAN DIVER AHMED GABR HOLDS THE RECORD FOR THE DEEPEST SCUBA DIVE, REACHING A DEPTH OF 1,090 FEET, 4.5 INCHES (332 METERS, 35 CENTIMETERS) IN SEPTEMBER 2014.

21. THERE ARE UNDERWATER LAKES AND RIVERS ON THE SEAFLOOR.

They form when dense pockets of particularly salty water settle into depressions on the seafloor.

22. THE OCEAN IS CURRENTLY LOSING SEAGRASS—A COASTAL MARINE PLANT THAT SOAKS UP CARBON POLLUTION—AT A RATE OF ONE SOCCER FIELD EVERY 30 MINUTES.

23. A STARFISH EATS BY PUSHING ITS STOMACH OUT OF ITS MOUTH AND USING IT TO ENVELOP ITS PREY.

24. ALGAE BLOOMS CAN CREATE MASSIVE "DEAD ZONES" WITHIN BODIES OF WATER.

When algae dies, the decomposition process leaves the nearby water deprived of oxygen, which can result in large die-offs of fish and other marine life.

25. THE WHITE SHELL OF THE MONEY COWRIE WAS USED AS CURRENCY AROUND THE WORLD FOR NEARLY 4,000 YEARS.

26. BELIEVE IT OR NOT, EDGAR ALLAN POE WROTE A GUIDE TO SEASHELLS TITLED *THE CONCHOLOGIST'S FIRST BOOK*.

Not only that, it was the only book of his to receive a second printing during his lifetime!

27. ALMOST ALL COILED SHELLS (SUCH AS SNAIL SHELLS) HAVE THEIR OPENING ON THE RIGHT-HAND SIDE.

Snails with "left-handed" shells find it difficult or impossible to mate—but their shells have become sought-after collector's items.

• 28 •

MANATEES HAVE A UNIQUE WAY OF ADJUSTING THEIR BUOYANCY: THEY FART!

· 29 ·

TIGER FISH CAN LEAP OUT OF THE WATER AND EAT FISH IN MIDAIR!

30. THANKS TO GLOBAL WARMING AND POLLUTION, THE EARTH HAS LOST APPROXIMATELY 50% OF ITS CORAL REEFS SINCE 1950.

31. MANATEES' NIPPLES ARE IN THEIR ARMPITS—OR RATHER, FLIPPERPITS.

32. TO AVOID PREDATORS AND WITHSTAND HEAVY PRESSURE DURING DEEP DIVES, THE MARINE IGUANA CAN SLOW ITS HEART RATE AND EVEN STOP IT FROM BEATING ENTIRELY.

33. HUMANS AREN'T THE ONLY CREATURES WHO FAKE ORGASMS: FEMALE TROUT HAVE BEEN OBSERVED PRETENDING TO RELEASE THEIR EGGS IN ORDER TO AVOID MATING WITH UNDESIRABLE MALES.

34. THANKS TO THE WATER CYCLE, THE WATER ON EARTH TODAY IS THE SAME WATER THAT HAS BEEN PRESENT FOR MILLIONS OF YEARS.

35. THE JAPANESE SPIDER CRAB IS THE LARGEST CRAB IN THE WORLD.

It can reach an astonishing 12 feet (almost 4 meters) from claw to claw and weigh over 42 pounds (19 kilograms)!

36. THE PINK SEE-THROUGH FANTASIA IS A TYPE OF SEA CUCUMBER, AND, AS ITS NAME IMPLIES, IT HAS TRANSPARENT SKIN THAT REVEALS ITS ENTIRE INTESTINAL TRACT.

Other names for this strange creature include the "headless chicken fish," the "headless chicken monster," and the "Spanish dancer."

37. SAWFISH HAVE HIGHLY SENSITIVE ELECTROMAGNETIC RECEPTORS THAT ALLOW THEM TO "FEEL" THE HEARTBEAT OF NEARBY PREY.

38. THE SNAKE ISN'T THE ONLY CREATURE CAPABLE OF CONSUMING VICTIMS LARGER THAN ITSELF: THE BLACK SWALLOWER IS A TYPE OF DEEP-SEA FISH CAPABLE OF SWALLOWING PREY 10 TIMES ITS MASS AND TWICE ITS LENGTH.

39. FISH DON'T HAVE EYELIDS, BUT THE GIANT GUITARFISH CAN PROTECT ITS EYES BY RETRACTING ITS EYEBALLS NEARLY 2 INCHES (5 CENTIMETERS) INSIDE ITS HEAD.

40. FISH HAVE TASTE BUDS NOT JUST ON THEIR TONGUES, BUT ON THE OUTSIDE OF THEIR BODIES AS WELL.

Some fish, including certain types of catfish, have taste receptors spread across their entire bodies.

· 41 ·

THE PARROTFISH STAYS SAFE BY SURROUNDING ITSELF WITH A BUBBLE OF ITS OWN MUCUS TO MASK ITS SCENT.

Yuck!

• 42 •

THE VIPER DOGFISH IS AN INCREDIBLY RARE DEEP-SEA FISH.

It emits its own light via tiny cells known as "photophores," and scientists believe that they use these to hunt their prey.

43. FLYING FISH DON'T ACTUALLY FLY—THEY GLIDE—WHICH MAKES IT EVEN MORE IMPRESSIVE THAT THE LONGEST KNOWN FLIGHT PERFORMED BY A FLYING FISH WAS AN INCREDIBLE 1,312 FEET (400 METERS)!

44. THE SLOWEST FISH IN THE WORLD IS THE DWARF SEAHORSE.

These little guys take an hour to move just 5 feet (1.5 meters)!

45. FUGU IS A TYPE OF PUFFER FISH CONSIDERED A DELICACY IN JAPAN AND OTHER PARTS OF ASIA.

However, fugu contains an incredibly powerful neurotoxin with no known antidote. If improperly prepared, it can kill anyone who consumes it—and between one and six people die each year from consuming fugu.

46. WHEN A HAGFISH RELEASES ITS SLIME, IT EXPANDS TO ROUGHLY 10,000 TIMES ITS ORIGINAL SIZE, OFTEN PRODUCING ENOUGH TO FILL A BUCKET!

47. LAMPREYS ARE OFTEN CONSIDERED "LIVING FOSSILS" BECAUSE OF HOW LITTLE THEY HAVE CHANGED IN THE LAST 500 MILLION YEARS.

48. CERTAIN TYPES OF FISH HAVE "TOOTHLIKE" SCALES THAT ARE APPROPRIATELY REFERRED TO AS "DENTICLES."

49. AS GLOBAL WARMING DESTROYS CORAL REEFS, MANY FISH ARE TAKING SHELTER IN AN UNUSUAL PLACE: SHIPWRECKS! SOME SCIENTISTS BELIEVE THAT THESE SHIPWRECKS MAY ACTUALLY HELP FISH ADAPT TO THE CHANGING CLIMATE.

50. BIGEYE THRESHER SHARKS CAN GROW UP TO 16 FEET (5 METERS) LONG, AND THEIR LONG TAILS ACCOUNT FOR HALF OF THEIR TOTAL BODY LENGTH.

They can whip their tails to stun or kill prey, or they've been known to circle a school of fish or squid, using their long tails to force prey closer together to make them easier to hunt.

51. SHORTFIN MAKO SHARKS ARE INCREDIBLE SHORT-AND LONG-DISTANCE SWIMMERS.

They travel an average of 36 miles (58 kilometers) every day and can accelerate up to 44 mph (71 kmh) in short bursts.

52. DESPITE BEING ONE OF THE LARGEST FISH IN THE WORLD (MEASURING UP TO 40 FEET—12 METERS—LONG!), THE WHALE SHARK IS NOT A PREDATOR, BUT A BOTTOM-FEEDER.

· 53 ·

DECORATOR CRABS REALLY EARN THEIR NAME: THEY CAMOUFLAGE THEMSELVES BY STICKING SEAWEED, ROCKS, AND OTHER SMALL OBJECTS TO THEIR SHELLS.

The bristles on the shells themselves
help keep these objects in place.

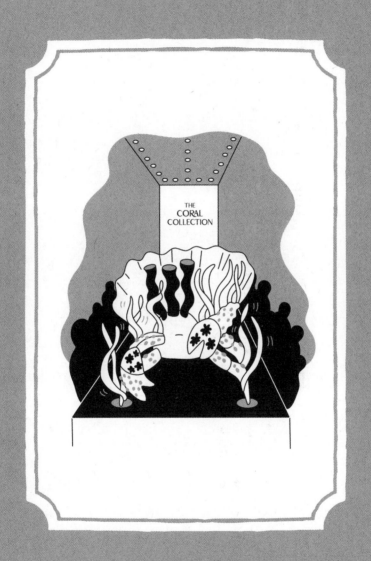

THE
CORAL
COLLECTION

· 54 ·

A SEAHORSE'S TAIL
ISN'T JUST FOR SHOW:
IT IS PREHENSILE AND
CAN BE USED TO GRAB
ON TO THINGS.

55. A BASKING SHARK'S STOMACH CAN HOLD NEARLY 1,100 POUNDS (NEARLY 500 KILOGRAMS) OF PLANKTON, WHICH IT OBTAINS BY SWIMMING AROUND WITH ITS MOUTH WIDE OPEN.

56. THE AREA JUST OVER THE OCEAN FLOOR IS KNOWN AS THE "ABYSSAL ZONE" OR SIMPLY "THE ABYSS."

The areas below the ocean floor (such as deep ocean trenches) are known as the "hadal zone," named for Hades, the Greek god of the underworld.

57. "ABYSSAL PLAINS" COVER MORE THAN HALF OF THE EARTH'S SURFACE.

These plains stretch from 10,000 feet to 20,000 feet (4,536 meters to 9,072 meters) below the ocean's surface, and they are considered the largest habitat on the planet. An astonishing amount of life survives on the abyssal plains!

58. THE LONGEST MOUNTAIN RANGE ON EARTH IS DEEP BELOW THE SURFACE OF THE OCEAN.

Known as a "mid-ocean ridge," the longest mountain range is over 40,000 miles (64,374 kilometers) from end to end!

59. MID-OCEAN RIDGES FORM VERY DIFFERENTLY FROM TRADITIONAL MOUNTAINS.

On land, two tectonic plates smash together and push upward, creating a mountain. Under the sea, tectonic plates pull apart, and magma gushes out. When it cools, it eventually forms an undersea mountain.

60. SOUTHERN SLEEPER SHARKS ARE AMONG THE MOST FEARSOME PREDATORS IN THE OCEAN.

Scientists have found the remains of giant squid in the stomachs of sleeper sharks, even though sleeper sharks are barely half their size!

61. THE FAMOUS SPIRAL SHELL OF THE NAUTILUS HELPS IT MOVE: THE GAS INSIDE ALLOWS IT TO RISE OR SINK, JUST LIKE A SUBMARINE.

62. *BOOPS BOOPS* IS THE REAL NAME OF A TYPE OF FISH IN THE EASTERN ATLANTIC OCEAN.

63. THE AXOLOTL IS AN AQUATIC SALAMANDER WITH A UNIQUE ABILITY: IT CAN REGENERATE ANY PART OF ITS BODY—INCLUDING ITS BRAIN.

64. IN 1992, A CARGO SHIP ACCIDENTALLY DROPPED A SHIPMENT OF 28,000 RUBBER DUCKS INTO THE OCEAN. BUT NOT ALL WAS LOST!

Tracking where the ducks ended up allowed oceanographers to better understand ocean currents.

65. OCEAN WATER HAS GOLD DISSOLVED IN IT: ROUGHLY ONE GRAM OF GOLD PER 100 MILLION METRIC TONS OF WATER.

That might not sound like much, but it amounts to more than $750 trillion worth of gold across all of Earth's oceans!

· 66 ·

THE PACU FISH HAS ONE VERY DISTURBING CHARACTERISTIC: ITS TEETH BEAR A STRONG RESEMBLANCE TO HUMAN TEETH.

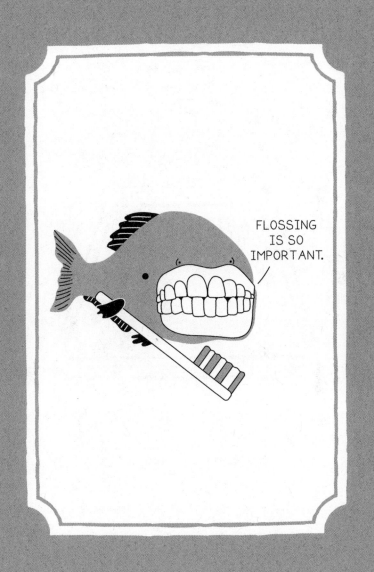

• 67 •

BOXER CRABS USE LIVING SEA ANEMONES AS "BOXING GLOVES."

It's a symbiotic relationship: the anemones use the crabs to get around, and the crabs use the anemones' stingers as weapons.

68. THERE IS A PHENOMENON KNOWN AS A "ROGUE WAVE," IN WHICH A MASSIVE WAVE WILL FORM SEEMINGLY OUT OF NOWHERE, WITH GREAT DESTRUCTIVE POTENTIAL.

Rogue waves pose a serious hazard to ships on the water.

69. ACCORDING TO SOME MEASUREMENTS, THE TALLEST ABOVEGROUND WATERFALL IN THE WORLD IS IN SOUTH AFRICA. TUGELA FALLS HAS AN ASTONISHING 3,225-FOOT (283-METER) DROP.

70. ONLY ABOUT 0.007% OF THE WATER ON EARTH IS USABLE BY HUMANS.

The rest is made up of salt water, glaciers, and otherwise inaccessible water.

71. THE "VAMPIRE SQUID" HAS A UNIQUE DEFENSE MECHANISM: IT TURNS ITSELF INSIDE OUT TO CONFUSE PREDATORS!

72. CRABS (OR CRAB-LIKE CREATURES) HAVE INDEPENDENTLY EVOLVED AT LEAST FIVE SEPARATE TIMES ON EARTH.

Scientists coined the term "carcinization" to describe this strange phenomenon and have joked that "everything eventually becomes a crab."

73. BY 2050, SCIENTISTS ESTIMATE THAT THERE WILL BE MORE PLASTIC IN THE EARTH'S OCEANS THAN FISH.

74. THE OCEAN CONTAINS SO MUCH SALT THAT IF YOU REMOVED IT AND SPREAD IT EVENLY ACROSS THE LAND, THE RESULTING LAYER OF SALT WOULD BE MORE THAN 500 FEET (152 METERS) DEEP!

75. IN 1997, OCEANOGRAPHERS RECORDED THE SOUND OF AN "ICEQUAKE" THAT THEY DUBBED "THE BLOOP."

It was one of the loudest sounds ever recorded, and for a long time scientists thought it might have been made by an enormous, undiscovered sea creature.

76. THE LARGEST WATERFALLS IN THE WORLD... IS UNDERWATER.

The Denmark Strait cataract is an undersea waterfall with a height of 11,500 feet (3,505 meters)!

77. WHEN DEEP-SEA ANGLERFISH MATE, THE SMALLER MALES PHYSICALLY FUSE THEMSELVES TO THE LARGER FEMALES—AND STAY THAT WAY FOR THE REST OF THEIR LIVES.

78. THERE ARE "BLACK HOLES" THAT EXIST UNDER THE OCEAN.

Certain ocean eddies can form closed loops of water from which nothing can escape.

• 79 •

A SHRIMP'S HEART IS LOCATED IN ITS HEAD!

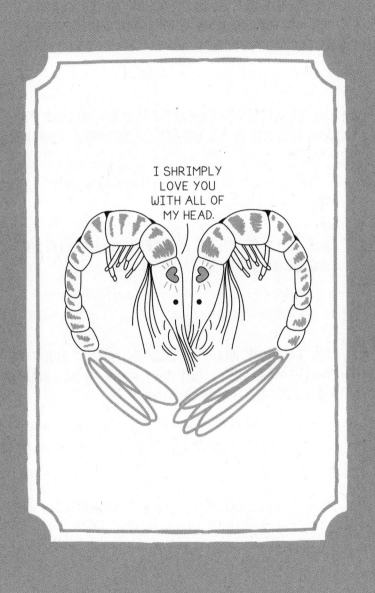

80. A SINGLE TABLESPOON OF OCEAN WATER CAN CONTAIN HUNDREDS OF THOUSANDS (MAYBE EVEN MILLIONS) OF VIRUSES.

Fortunately, most are not harmful to humans.

81. TRUE OR FALSE: THE SARCASTIC FRINGEHEAD GETS ITS NAME BECAUSE OF ITS SNEAKY, BACKHANDED BEHAVIOR.

False. The sarcastic fringehead is a real fish—but it gets its name because it has a big mouth and lashes out at anything and everything nearby.

82. TRUE OR FALSE: THERE IS A SPECIES OF JELLYFISH THAT LOOKS JUST LIKE A FRIED EGG.

True. The appropriately named fried egg jellyfish has a whitish body with a yellow, circular center.

83. TRUE OR FALSE: GIANT CLAMS ARE "GIANT" RELATIVE TO OTHER MOLLUSKS, BUT ONLY GROW TO BE ABOUT 6 INCHES (15 CENTIMETERS) ACROSS.

False. Giant clams really do live up to their name: the largest ones can be almost 4 feet (one meter) across and weigh more than 500 pounds (227 kilograms)!

84. TRUE OR FALSE: ELECTRIC EELS ARE NOT ACTUALLY EELS.

True. They technically have more in common with catfish than eels!

85. TRUE OR FALSE: THERE IS A RIVER IN THE AMAZON WHERE THE WATER NATURALLY BOILS.

True. Well, sort of. It isn't quite "boiling," but the water temperatures in the Shanay-Timpishka River can reach more than 200 degrees Fahrenheit (93 degrees Celsius), effectively cooking any wildlife unlucky enough to fall in.

86. TRUE OR FALSE: THE DENSITY OF THE DEAD SEA IS SO LOW THAT HUMANS IMMEDIATELY SINK TO THE BOTTOM.

False. Exactly the opposite. The water is so salty and dense that humans float with no trouble whatsoever.

87. TRUE OR FALSE: THE GREAT BARRIER REEF CAN BE SEEN FROM THE MOON.

True. It's one of the few objects on Earth that can stake that claim.

88. TRUE OR FALSE: THE LONGEST ANY FISH CAN SURVIVE ON LAND IS 12 HOURS.

False. By a lot! The African lungfish can wrap itself in a mucus-like cocoon that allows it to survive on land for up to an entire year!

89. TRUE OR FALSE: THE SAHARA DESERT WAS ONCE UNDERWATER.

True. Not the entire desert, perhaps—but significant chunks of it. The Sahara is a surprisingly rich source of undersea fossils.

· 90 ·

TRUE OR FALSE:
FISH CAN GET SUNBURNED.

True. Strange as it sounds, fish can become
sunburned. Fish that live in shallow water,
such as koi and other backyard varieties, are
particularly susceptible.

· 91 ·

TRUE OR FALSE: IT TAKES AROUND 1,000 YEARS FOR WATER TO CIRCUMNAVIGATE THE GLOBE.

True. The "global ocean conveyor belt" is a system of currents that circulates water around the globe. Scientists estimate that it takes about 1,000 years for water to make a full cycle.

92. TRUE OR FALSE: CORAL IS SO SIMILAR TO HUMAN BONE THAT IT CAN BE USED IN BONE GRAFTS.

True. The discovery was made by a scuba-diving professor in the 1980s!

93. TRUE OR FALSE: ON AVERAGE, SHARKS KILL MORE THAN 100 HUMANS EVERY YEAR.

False. In a typical year, only between five and ten people are killed by sharks. They're much less deadly than you might think!

94. TRUE OR FALSE: ONE LAKE HOLDS 20% OF THE WORLD'S FRESH WATER.

True. Russia's Lake Baikal is the largest freshwater lake in the world. In fact, it holds an incredible 20% of the planet's unfrozen fresh water.

95. TRUE OR FALSE: IN THE DEEPEST PARTS OF THE OCEAN, THE PRESSURE IS TOO GREAT TO SUSTAIN MARINE LIFE, MAKING THEM EERILY LIFELESS.

False. In fact, the bottom of the ocean is still teeming with life. Fish have been observed swimming at incredible depths within the Mariana Trench itself.

96. TRUE OR FALSE: JELLYFISH ARE 60% WATER.

False. Actually, jellyfish are 95% water. They don't have a brain or a heart, and they have no blood!

97. TRUE OR FALSE: MORE PEOPLE HAVE BEEN TO THE MOON THAN HAVE BEEN TO THE BOTTOM OF THE MARIANA TRENCH.

True. Only three people have ever reached the lowest parts of the ocean, while 12 human beings have set foot on the moon.

98. TRUE OR FALSE: SCIENTISTS HAVE FOUND THAT SHARK EMBRYOS ENGAGE IN COOPERATIVE BEHAVIOR WITH ONE ANOTHER BEFORE EVEN BEING BORN.

False. In fact, scientists have observed embryos cannibalizing one another while still in the womb.

99. TRUE OR FALSE: IF ALL OF THE ICE CAPS AND GLACIERS MELTED, THE EARTH'S SEA LEVEL WOULD RISE ABOUT 15 FEET (4.6 METERS).

False. If that happened, the sea level would rise over 200 feet (61 meters)—more than enough to wipe out most coastal cities. Letting the ice caps melt would be a very bad idea!

· 100 ·

TRUE OR FALSE:
OVER 50% OF THE LAKES
AND RIVERS IN THE UNITED
STATES ARE TOO POLLUTED
FOR SWIMMING, DRINKING,
OR FISHING.

True. Unfortunately. Given how little
fresh water is accessible to humans,
the problem of water pollution is a
significant one.

Human Anatomy & Biology

What could be more natural than the human body, right? We all have one, and we know it well. Or do we? You might be surprised to learn a few of the lesser-known facts about the human body. For instance, did you know that you have more than five senses? Or that your tongueprint is as unique as your fingerprint? How about the fact that you can taste garlic with your feet? Yes, the human body is an amazing (and terrifying!) thing.

1. EVERYONE KNOWS ABOUT NEANDERTHALS, BUT DID YOU KNOW THAT SCIENTISTS HAVE DISCOVERED AT LEAST 20 OTHER DISTINCT HUMAN SPECIES THROUGHOUT HISTORY?

2. THERE IS A CONDITION CALLED "SITUS INVERSUS," IN WHICH THE POSITION OF A HUMAN'S ABDOMINAL ORGANS (LUNGS, HEART, LIVER, ETC.) ARE REVERSED WITHIN THE BODY.

3. THE AVERAGE HUMAN PRODUCES OVER 20,000 LITERS OF SALIVA IN THEIR LIFETIME.

4. YOU ARE TALLER IN THE MORNING THAN YOU ARE AT NIGHT.

5. A 1997 STUDY FOUND THAT THE AVERAGE FART CONTAINS BETWEEN 17 MILLILITERS AND 375 MILLILITERS OF AIR.

6. THE REASON CUTTING ONIONS MAKES YOU CRY IS THAT THE GAS RELEASED BY A SLICED ONION COMBINES WITH THE WATER IN YOUR EYES TO FORM SULFURIC ACID.

7. SCIENTISTS ESTIMATE THAT THE HUMAN BRAIN CONTAINS 85 BILLION NEURONS.

8. NOT EVERYONE CAN SMELL SO-CALLED "ASPARAGUS PEE."

Like the ability to taste cilantro, this smelling ability is driven by genetic differences.

9. THE CELLS THAT MAKE UP YOUR SKIN COMPLETELY REGENERATE EVERY 27 OR SO DAYS.

As humans age, this process begins to take longer.

10. WHEN YOU'RE STRESSED, IT CAN HAVE A NEGATIVE EFFECT ON YOUR DIGESTIVE SYSTEM.

11. SOME WOMEN HAVE A CONDITION KNOWN AS "UTERUS DIDELPHYS," IN WHICH THEY ARE BORN WITH TWO SEPARATE UTERUSES.

12. THE LONGEST RECORDED PREGNANCY LASTED 375 DAYS—ALMOST 100 DAYS LONGER THAN AVERAGE! IT TOPS THE SECOND-LONGEST PREGNANCY BY 58 DAYS.

13. *DEMODEX* MITES LIVE ON THE FACE OF ALMOST EVERY HUMAN.

Don't worry, though—they're almost entirely harmless, and actually help by removing dead skin cells!

• 14 •

THE AVERAGE HUMAN SHEDS APPROXIMATELY 500 MILLION DEAD SKIN CELLS EVERY DAY.

• 15 •

WHEN YOU BLUSH, IT
ISN'T JUST YOUR CHEEKS
THAT TURN RED: THE
LINING OF YOUR STOMACH
TURNS RED TOO.

16. ALTHOUGH IT IS COMMONLY BELIEVED THAT THE HUMAN NOSE AND EARS NEVER STOP GROWING, THIS IS NOT EXACTLY TRUE.

The nose and ears are made primarily of cartilage, and while cartilage does stop growing, it is more susceptible to the effects of gravity. As a result, the nose and ears may continue to lengthen over time.

17. YOUR STOMACH LINING REGENERATES EVERY FIVE TO SEVEN DAYS. IF IT DIDN'T, YOUR STOMACH WOULD EVENTUALLY START TO DIGEST ITSELF!

18. THE RESOLUTION OF THE HUMAN EYE IS 576 MEGAPIXELS.

19. THE AVERAGE HUMAN WILL GROW 590 MILES (950 KILOMETERS) OF HAIR OVER THE COURSE OF THEIR LIFETIME. (LAID END TO END, OF COURSE.)

20. YOUR FINGERNAILS GROW MUCH FASTER THAN YOUR TOENAILS, THOUGH NO ONE IS SURE WHY. ONE THEORY IS THAT THE FINGERS ARE CLOSER TO THE HEART, AND THEREFORE RECEIVE MORE BLOOD.

21. THE HUMAN BRAIN IS APPROXIMATELY 60% FAT!

22. THE PINKIE FINGER DOESN'T GET NEARLY ENOUGH RESPECT. SCIENTISTS ESTIMATE THAT THE PINKIE IS RESPONSIBLE FOR ROUGHLY A THIRD OF YOUR GRIP STRENGTH!

23. DESPITE THE COMMON BELIEF THAT SUGAR CAUSES HYPERACTIVITY IN CHILDREN, QUITE A BIT OF RESEARCH NOW SHOWS THAT THERE IS LITTLE TO NO CONNECTION BETWEEN THE TWO.

24. ACCORDING TO SCIENTISTS, HUMANS ACTUALLY HAVE MORE THAN FIVE SENSES.

In addition to sight, hearing, smell, taste, and touch, humans also have "exteroceptive" senses. One example is "interoception," which allows you to sense the things happening inside your body (rumbling stomach, beating heart, etc.). Some argue that your sense of balance and ability to feel the passage of time are also senses.

25. YOUR INTESTINES NEVER STOP MOVING.

They engage in a continuous, wavy movement known as "peristalsis" that helps move food through your digestive system.

• 26 •

THE AVERAGE ADULT HUMAN HAS MORE THAN 60,000 MILES (96,561 KILOMETERS) OF BLOOD VESSELS INSIDE THEIR BODY.

That's more than double the circumference of the Earth!

• 27 •

YOUR "TONGUEPRINT" IS AS UNIQUE AS YOUR FINGERPRINT—BUT WE PROBABLY WON'T START RECORDING TONGUEPRINTS ANYTIME SOON.

28. NO ONE KNOWS WHY WE NEED SLEEP.

Scientists speculate that it plays some sort of restorative role, but no one can say for certain why sleep is biologically necessary.

29. THE HUMAN LIVER CAN REGROW TO ITS NORMAL SIZE EVEN AFTER 90% OF IT HAS BEEN REMOVED!

It is the only organ that can regenerate itself after being damaged.

30. TWINS DON'T JUST LOOK IDENTICAL.

They smell identical too. It turns out that human body odor is closely tied to genetics!

31. A TERATOMA IS A RARE TYPE OF TUMOR WHICH CAN CONTAIN A WIDE VARIETY OF DIFFERENT TISSUE TYPES...

including muscle, bone, teeth, and hair. Gross!

32. BABIES ONLY BLINK ONCE OR TWICE PER MINUTE— MUCH LESS FREQUENTLY THAN ADULTS, WHO AVERAGE ABOUT 12-15 TIMES PER MINUTE.

33. IN 2021, A WOMAN IN MOROCCO GAVE BIRTH TO NINE BABIES—THE FIRST RECORDED CASE OF NONUPLETS IN WHICH ALL NINE CHILDREN SURVIVED.

34. THERE ARE ABOUT 10,000 DIFFERENT SPECIES OF MICROBES LIVING ON YOUR BODY RIGHT NOW.

35. ON AVERAGE, YOUR SKIN ACCOUNTS FOR 15% OF YOUR TOTAL BODY WEIGHT.

That's a lot of skin!

36. HUMANS ARE THE ONLY ANIMALS THAT SHED TEARS FOR EMOTIONAL REASONS—AND SCIENTISTS DON'T FULLY UNDERSTAND WHY.

37. EVER WONDERED WHY YOUR FOOD PREFERENCES CHANGE OVER TIME?

It may have something to do with the fact that humans lose roughly one-third of their taste buds between infancy and adulthood.

38. THE HUMAN BRAIN CANNOT FEEL PAIN. IT HAS NO PAIN RECEPTORS AT ALL!

39. BECAUSE THE BRAIN HAS NO PAIN RECEPTORS, BRAIN SURGERY CAN BE PERFORMED WHILE THE PATIENT IS AWAKE.

In fact, brain surgeons often prefer to operate this way, as it is believed to be safer.

· 40 ·

YOU CAN TASTE AND SMELL GARLIC...WITH YOUR FEET.

Garlic contains a molecule that can permeate the skin of your feet and travel all the way to your mouth and nose via the bloodstream.

• 41 •

YOUR BODY GLOWS
IN THE DARK!

Unfortunately, the bioluminescence
produced by the human body is extremely
weak—about 1,000 times weaker than the
human eye can detect.

42. THERE IS A DISORDER KNOWN AS "SUPERIOR CANAL DEHISCENCE SYNDROME" THAT AMPLIFIES INTERNAL BODY SOUNDS FOR THOSE WHO SUFFER FROM IT.

People with SCDS often have the unsettling experience of listening to their own eyeballs moving in their sockets.

43. THE TONGUE IS REFERRED TO AS THE STRONGEST MUSCLE IN THE BODY, BUT IN ACTUALITY YOUR TONGUE IS MADE UP OF EIGHT DIFFERENT MUSCLES!

44. WHEN WALKING NORMALLY, YOUR BIG TOE BEARS ABOUT 40% OF YOUR BODY WEIGHT.

That's a strong toe!

45. YOUR EYE COLOR CAN INDICATE YOUR ALCOHOL TOLERANCE.

People with blue eyes tend to take longer to feel the effects of alcohol. However, those with blue eyes may also have higher rates of alcoholism.

46. DESPITE WHAT YOU MAY THINK, YOUR SWEAT IS ODORLESS!

That body-odor smell is actually caused by the bacteria on your skin interacting with the chemicals in your sweat.

47. THE HUMAN BRAIN OPERATES ON ABOUT 10-15 WATTS OF ELECTRICAL ENERGY.

Now that's an efficient computer!

48. YOUR BRAIN MAKES UP ONLY ABOUT 2% OF YOUR BODY WEIGHT, BUT IT USES 20% OF YOUR BODY'S ENERGY.

49. IF YOU HAVE THIN HAIR, DON'T WORRY! SCIENTISTS HAVE FOUND THAT THIN HAIR IS MEASURABLY STRONGER THAN THICK HAIR.

50. LOW-GRAVITY ENVIRONMENTS CAN HAVE A STRANGE EFFECT ON THE HUMAN BODY.

Astronauts' blood will occasionally run backwards when they are working in zero gravity!

51. MOST PEOPLE HAVE HEARD THE TERM "TOENAIL FUNGUS."

Well, almost 200 types of fungi are living on your feet at any given time. That said, most are harmless...unless poor hygiene allows them to grow out of control.

52. HUMANS ARE SOMETIMES REFERRED TO AS "NAKED APES" BECAUSE WE APPEAR MUCH LESS HAIRY THAN OTHER PRIMATES.

But that's not really true—humans have as many hair follicles per square centimeter as other, similar primates, but our hair is much finer and less visible.

· 53 ·

WHEN TWO PEOPLE WHO LOVE EACH OTHER ARE IN CLOSE PROXIMITY, THEIR HEARTBEATS CAN SYNC UP.

Your hearts literally beat for each other!

• 54 •

YOU HAVE TASTE RECEPTORS IN YOUR KIDNEYS.

Scientists aren't quite sure what function they serve.

55. HUMANS CAN DIE FROM DRINKING TOO MUCH WATER.

But don't worry—you would have to drink a LOT of water to succumb to water poisoning, and cases are incredibly rare.

56. THE AVERAGE HUMAN PRODUCES ABOUT 1.5 QUARTS (1.4 LITERS) OF MUCUS A DAY.

Where does it go? Bad news: you swallow most of it.

57. OF THE CELLS THAT MAKE UP YOUR BODY, LESS THAN HALF ARE "HUMAN" CELLS.

The rest are bacterial cells of various types.

58. WHEN A HUMAN RECEIVES A TRANSPLANTED KIDNEY, DOCTORS USUALLY DON'T BOTHER REMOVING THE OLD KIDNEY (UNLESS IT IS CAUSING A SPECIFIC PROBLEM).

As a result, some people are walking around with three kidneys. Some even have four!

59. WHEN YOUR STOMACH RUMBLES, THE SOUND ISN'T ACTUALLY COMING FROM YOUR STOMACH.

Usually, it originates in the small intestine.

60. WHEN YOU ARE STRESSED OR WORRIED, YOU PRODUCE MORE EARWAX THAN USUAL.

61. WHY DOES SEEING SOMEONE ELSE VOMIT MAKE YOU WANT TO VOMIT?

Scientists think it may have evolved as a protection against food poisoning, prompting other nearby humans who may have eaten the same food to purge it from their bodies.

62. YOU CAN BREAK A RIB JUST BY COUGHING OR SNEEZING.

But don't worry—the cough or sneeze would have to be particularly severe for that to happen.

63. "OLD-PERSON SMELL" IS REAL.

But the truth is, studies have shown that humans just smell different at various stages of life.

64. SOMEWHERE BETWEEN 8% AND 10% OF YOUR BODY WEIGHT...IS BLOOD.

65. THERE IS A CONDITION KNOWN AS "EXPLODING HEAD SYNDROME" THAT CAUSES SUFFERERS TO HEAR A LOUD "BANG" IN THEIR HEADS WHEN THEY WAKE UP (AND SOMETIMES WHEN THEY FALL ASLEEP TOO).

66. PASSING GAS IS AN IMPORTANT INDICATOR OF NORMAL GUT FUNCTION FOLLOWING A C-SECTION.

In fact, if you've had a C-section, doctors often won't let you eat until you fart!

• 67 •

IT TURNS OUT THAT YOUR HANDS ARE PRETTY GROSS.

The average handshake transfers more germs than a kiss!

· 68 ·

THE LOUDEST BURP EVER RECORDED BY A HUMAN WAS 112.4 DECIBELS.

That's louder than most car horns!

69. YOUR BONES ARE ACTUALLY NOT FULLY SOLID.

In addition to being filled with spongy bone marrow, they have tiny holes to allow blood vessels and nerves in.

70. SOME PEOPLE SNEEZE AS AN INVOLUNTARY REACTION TO SEXUAL AROUSAL.

This "sexually induced sneezing" can be very awkward!

71. IF A PREGNANT WOMAN IS INJURED, THE FETUS INSIDE HER WILL SOMETIMES "DONATE" ITS OWN STEM CELLS TO AID IN THE HEALING PROCESS.

72. THE HUMAN BODY HAS SAFEGUARDS IN PLACE TO STOP YOU FROM USING ALL OF YOUR STRENGTH.

This block can be overridden during dire situations, which is why a mother might, for example, be able to lift a car off of her trapped child.

73. THERE IS A RARE, INCURABLE CONDITION CALLED MÜNCHMEYER'S DISEASE, IN WHICH THE VICTIM'S MUSCLES, TENDONS, AND LIGAMENTS ALL SLOWLY TURN TO BONE.

If the new bone growths are surgically removed, the body simply replaces them with more bone.

74. SOME PEOPLE COUGH WHEN SOMETHING ENTERS THEIR EAR CANAL.

The condition is called "Arnold's nerve ear-cough reflex" and is believed to be benign.

75. A SINGLE VOXEL (THE 3D EQUIVALENT OF A PIXEL) IN AN MRI CONTAINS BETWEEN ONE MILLION AND THREE MILLION NEURONS.

How much do we really know about the brain?

76. RESEARCHERS HAVE FOUND THAT MEN WHO LOSE A SPOUSE ARE 70% MORE LIKELY TO DIE WITHIN A YEAR, WHILE WOMEN WHO LOSE A SPOUSE ARE JUST 27% MORE LIKELY TO DIE.

77. THE PLACEBO EFFECT IS SO POWERFUL THAT IT CAN WORK EVEN WHEN THE PATIENT KNOWS THAT THEY ARE TAKING A PLACEBO.

78. THE BONES IN YOUR BODY REGENERATE ABOUT EVERY 10 YEARS, WHICH MEANS THAT YOU GET A COMPLETELY NEW SKELETON EACH DECADE!

79. TAKING UP DRAWING HAS BEEN SHOWN TO SIGNIFICANTLY IMPROVE MEMORY RETENTION.

· 80 ·

YOUR EYES EXIST IN A "BLIND SPOT" WITHIN YOUR IMMUNE SYSTEM.

If your immune system suddenly became aware of your eyes, it would attack them as if they were a foreign body.

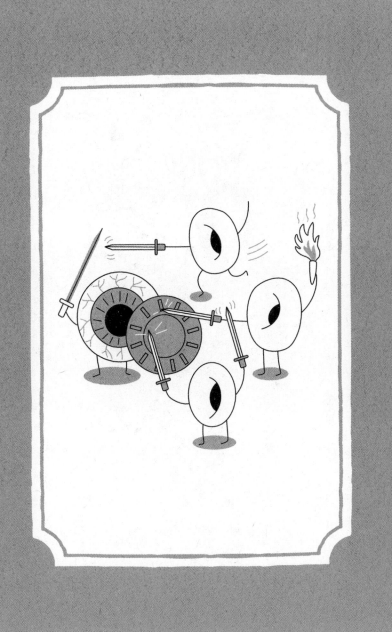

· 81 ·

TRUE OR FALSE: DOCTORS SAY IT IS EXTREMELY DANGEROUS TO WAKE A SLEEPWALKER.

False. Despite the common belief that waking a sleepwalker can cause them to have a heart attack or suffer a similar medical emergency, doctors agree that waking a sleepwalker is perfectly safe.

82. TRUE OR FALSE: DEOXYGENATED BLOOD APPEARS BLUE.

False. Your blood remains red no matter how much oxygen it contains. However, because of the way light travels through the skin, dark-red veins appear to be blue—leading to this common misconception.

83. TRUE OR FALSE: WHEN WOMEN LIVE TOGETHER, THEIR MENSTRUAL CYCLES EVENTUALLY SYNCHRONIZE.

False. This claim was first made in 1971, and it remains commonly believed to this day. However, evidence gathered since then appears to indicate that this is a myth.

84. TRUE OR FALSE: HUMAN BEINGS ARE DESCENDED FROM APES.

False. Don't worry, we're not about to disprove evolution. However, it is inaccurate to say human beings are descended from apes. In reality, humans and apes share a common ancestor, which humans would perceive as being more "apelike" than "humanlike."

85. TRUE OR FALSE: HUMAN URINE IS STERILE.

False. Despite the persistent myth that urine is sterile, the truth is that nothing that comes out of your body is sterile.

86. TRUE OR FALSE: HUMAN TEETH BECAME SMALLER AS OUR BRAINS GOT BIGGER.

False. Scientists believed for a long time that there was a connection between brain size and tooth size, but recent studies have disproven that hypothesis.

87. TRUE OR FALSE: YOU HAVE NO MUSCLES IN YOUR FINGERS.

True. Believe it or not, all of the muscles that control finger movement are located in your hand and forearm.

88. TRUE OR FALSE: HUMANS HAVE INVISIBLE STRIPES.

True. Blaschko's lines are invisible stripes related to the way human cells develop. They can be seen under ultraviolet light and can become visible on humans with certain skin conditions.

89. TRUE OR FALSE: BLIND HUMANS TEND TO HAVE BETTER MEMORIES.

False. In fact, just the opposite is true. Scientists have found that blindness can have a negative effect on memory and attention.

90. TRUE OR FALSE: ABOUT 8% OF OUR DNA COMES FROM VIRUSES THAT INFECTED ANCIENT HUMANS.

True. Over time, fighting off viruses has resulted in significant changes to human DNA.

• 91 •

TRUE OR FALSE: LIKE BATS, HUMAN BEINGS ARE CAPABLE OF ECHOLOCATION.

True. In multiple studies, blind humans have been taught to effectively navigate their surroundings by clicking their tongues and listening for the echo.

• 92 •

TRUE OR FALSE: IT IS POSSIBLE TO BE ALLERGIC TO WATER.

True. People with the rare condition "aquagenic urticaria" receive a red, irritated rash when they come into contact with water. Obviously, this makes daily life extremely difficult. Technically, it isn't an "allergy" in the strict, scientific sense, but it is an immune reaction commonly referred to as water allergy.

93. TRUE OR FALSE: WHEN YOU LOSE WEIGHT, EXCESS FAT IS EXPELLED THROUGH YOUR DIGESTIVE TRACT.

False. In fact, fat is broken down into water and carbon dioxide. The carbon dioxide is exhaled, while the water comes out as urine or sweat. Is it any wonder weight loss is so difficult?

94. TRUE OR FALSE: YOU CAN LIVE A RELATIVELY NORMAL LIFE WITH ONLY HALF OF YOUR BRAIN.

True. The brain is surprisingly adaptable, and the remaining half of the brain will often compensate by taking on responsibilities usually reserved for the other half. However, this gets harder as you age, and the removal procedure is usually carried out only as a last resort for children.

95. TRUE OR FALSE: THE HUMAN NOSE CAN DETECT MORE THAN ONE TRILLION DIFFERENT ODORS.

True. Believe it or not, that's a real fact. The human nose is truly amazing.

96. TRUE OR FALSE: REDHEADS ARE EASIER TO PUT UNDER ANESTHESIA THAN OTHERS.

False. Actually, redheads are harder to put under anesthesia. Studies have shown that redheads often require as much as 20% more anesthesia to remain sedated.

97. TRUE OR FALSE: SCIENTISTS DO NOT KNOW WHY HUMANS EVOLVED WITH EYEBROWS.

False. We're pretty sure the primary function of your eyebrows is to keep water (usually in the form of rain or sweat) out of your eyes. However, scientists believe that they also evolved to play a critical role in communication.

98. TRUE OR FALSE: YOU DO MOST OF YOUR BREATHING THROUGH ONE NOSTRIL AT A TIME.

True. No one is quite sure why, but you breathe significantly more through one nostril than the other. Even stranger, the "dominant nostril" switches every couple of hours.

99. TRUE OR FALSE: INFANTS DON'T HAVE KNEECAPS.

True. Don't worry, their knees aren't totally unprotected: infants have cartilage that keeps their knees safe. That cartilage turns to bone sometime between age 2 and age 6.

100. TRUE OR FALSE: IT IS POSSIBLE TO ACCIDENTALLY SWALLOW YOUR OWN TONGUE.

False. "Swallowing your tongue" is a common turn of phrase, but in reality there are many safeguards that prevent you from being able to swallow your tongue.

[The Natural World]

There's an old vocabulary game that begins with the question, "Animal, vegetable, or mineral?" Well, we've gone through the animals, and we've gone through the vegetables, so that leaves the minerals—among other things. Things like weather patterns, rock formations, and supercontinents may not fit neatly into a specific category, but they're part of nature nonetheless—and this section will provide the opportunity to learn more about all of them.

1. COWS AND OTHER LIVESTOCK ARE RESPONSIBLE FOR ROUGHLY 40% OF GLOBAL METHANE EMISSIONS, MAKING THEM A SIGNIFICANT DRIVER OF CLIMATE CHANGE.

2. WHILE THE "NORTHERN LIGHTS" (AURORA BOREALIS) ARE MORE WELL-KNOWN, THERE ARE "SOUTHERN LIGHTS" AS WELL, DUBBED THE AURORA AUSTRALIS.

3. THE GRAND CANYON IS BIGGER THAN THE ENTIRE STATE OF RHODE ISLAND.

4. LAKE HILLIER IS AN AUSTRALIAN BODY OF WATER WITH A STRANGE, PINK COLORATION.

Scientists believe that the color is due to the presence of a type of algae known as *Dunaliella salina*.

5. THE "DOOR TO HELL" IS A GAS CRATER IN TURKMENISTAN THAT HAS BEEN CONTINUOUSLY BURNING SINCE 1971.

6. THE LONGEST LIGHTNING BOLT OF ALL TIME WAS RECORDED IN 2020.

It stretched 477 miles (768 kilometers) across three different US states!

7. THE 2022 ERUPTION OF THE HUNGA TONGA VOLCANO CREATED THE LARGEST EXPLOSION EVER RECORDED ON EARTH.

It released more energy than even the most powerful nuclear bomb tests!

8. YOU CAN TELL THE TEMPERATURE BY COUNTING A CRICKET'S CHIRPS.

Count how many times a cricket chirps in 15 seconds and add 40—the sum is usually within a few degrees of the temperature (in Fahrenheit). This is called Dolbear's law, after Amos Dolbear, who published his observations in 1897.

9. ONE INCH (2.5 CENTIMETERS) OF RAIN IS EQUIVALENT TO 10 OR MORE INCHES (25 OR MORE CENTIMETERS) OF SNOW.

10. IT USUALLY TAKES BETWEEN 500 YEARS AND 1,000 YEARS FOR TOPSOIL TO FORM NATURALLY.

11. THERE IS ACTUALLY A FIFTH FORM OF MATTER, IN ADDITION TO SOLID, LIQUID, GAS, AND PLASMA.

A Bose-Einstein condensate (BEC) is a difficult-to-achieve state that occurs when matter approaches absolute zero—the temperature at which molecular motion stops. It could use a catchier name!

• 12 •

DESPITE HOW IT IS PORTRAYED IN THE MEDIA, IT IS ALMOST IMPOSSIBLE TO DIE IN QUICKSAND.

Because quicksand is denser than the human body, you might get stuck, but you won't sink to the bottom.

A COAL-MINE FIRE HAS BEEN BURNING BENEATH THE TOWN OF CENTRALIA, PENNSYLVANIA, SINCE 1962.

The town's population has plummeted over that time, with just five residents remaining as of 2020.

14. ITALY'S GAIOLA ISLAND, OFF THE COAST OF NAPLES, IS BELIEVED TO BE CURSED.

The reason? Every one of the island's owners since the start of the twentieth century has met a tragic fate. Past owners have drowned, been murdered, committed suicide, met financial ruin, or been imprisoned. Today, the island is owned by the local government.

15. ON AN AVERAGE DAY, THERE ARE OVER EIGHT MILLION LIGHTNING STRIKES RECORDED ACROSS THE PLANET EARTH.

16. SOME ANIMALS ARE BELIEVED TO HAVE MIGRATED BETWEEN LANDMASSES ON FLOATING "RAFTS" MADE FROM ROCK!

Because pumice floats, scientists believe that small rafts made of pumice have helped ferry animal life between islands.

17. RUBIES AND SAPPHIRES ARE TECHNICALLY THE SAME MINERAL.

Corundum can come in a range of colors—when it is red, it is called a ruby, and when it is blue, it is called a sapphire.

18. THE CITY OF CALAMA IN CHILE DID NOT RECEIVE A SINGLE DROP OF RAIN BETWEEN 1570 AND 1971—A DROUGHT STRETCHING OVER 400 YEARS!

19. HAWAII AND JAPAN ARE GETTING CLOSER TOGETHER...

but very slowly. Thanks to plate tectonics, Hawaii and Japan move 1.6 inches (4.1 centimeters) closer with each passing year.

20. ATOMS ARE ROUGHLY 99.9999999% EMPTY SPACE.

The actual protons, neutrons, and electrons within the atoms in your body make up just a tiny fraction of the space you occupy.

21. ASTATINE IS THE RAREST NATURALLY OCCURRING ELEMENT ON EARTH.

At any given time, it is believed that there are fewer than 30 grams present in Earth's crust.

22. THE MPEMBA EFFECT DESCRIBES A PHENOMENON IN WHICH HOT WATER SOMETIMES FREEZES MORE QUICKLY THAN COLD WATER.

23. WATER IS THE ONLY KNOWN (NONMETAL) SUBSTANCE THAT EXPANDS WHEN IT FREEZES.

24. SCIENTISTS HAVE DISCOVERED A SURPRISING PROPERTY OF DNA: IT APPEARS TO BE FIREPROOF!

· 25 ·

SOME SCIENTISTS BELIEVE THAT MOST (OR ALL) OF THE WATER ON EARTH WAS DEPOSITED BY COMETS AND ASTEROIDS DURING THE PERIOD KNOWN AS THE LATE HEAVY BOMBARDMENT.

· 26 ·

THE LARGEST SNOWFLAKE EVER RECORDED WAS 15 INCHES (38 CENTIMETERS) WIDE.

Perhaps even more amazing is the fact that it was 8 inches (20 centimeters) thick!

27. **HELIUM WILL NEVER FREEZE SOLID UNDER NORMAL CIRCUMSTANCES—EVEN IF YOU COOL IT TO ABSOLUTE ZERO!**

Only after being subjected to pressure of at least 20 atmospheres will helium become solid.

28. **AT ANY GIVEN TIME, MORE THAN TWO-THIRDS OF THE EARTH IS COVERED BY CLOUDS.**

29. **THE INDIAN TOWN OF MAWSYNRAM IS KNOWN AS THE "WETTEST PLACE ON EARTH," RECEIVING AN AVERAGE OF 467 INCHES (1,186 CENTIMETERS) OF RAIN PER YEAR.**

That's almost 39 feet (12 meters) of rain!

30. **IN 1996, A WEATHER STATION IN AUSTRALIA MEASURED A WIND GUST OF 253 MPH (407 KMH)—THE HIGHEST WIND SPEED ON RECORD!**

31. **MEN ARE FOUR TIMES AS LIKELY TO BE STRUCK BY LIGHTNING AS WOMEN.**

However, this is believed to be due to the fact that men generally spend more time outside and are more willing to engage in risky behavior.

32. **AN AVERAGE CUMULUS CLOUD WEIGHS APPROXIMATELY 1.1 MILLION POUNDS (500,000 KILOGRAMS).**

33. IN 1992, FOLLOWING A PERIOD OF PROLONGED SNOWFALL, THE CITY OF SYRACUSE, NEW YORK, PASSED A RESOLUTION MAKING ANY MORE SNOW BEFORE CHRISTMAS EVE ILLEGAL.

Sadly, Mother Nature did not comply.

34. SNOW CAN BE PINK!

In certain regions, snow can sometimes contain a type of red-tinted algae that gives the snow a pinkish hue. The phenomenon is often referred to as "watermelon snow."

35. YOU KNOW THE CLASSIC "RAINDROP" SHAPE?

Rain doesn't actually look like that. In fact, raindrops are mostly spherical until they encounter air resistance, which flattens the bottom and gives it a shape like a hamburger bun.

36. ULURU (ALSO KNOWN AS AYERS ROCK) IS THE LARGEST MONOLITH IN THE WORLD.

This massive sandstone formation is over 1,100 feet (335 meters) tall and almost 6 miles (10 kilometers) around!

37. WHEN YOU THINK "DESERT," YOU PROBABLY THINK SAND—BUT IN REALITY, ONLY ABOUT 20% OF EARTH'S DESERTS ARE COVERED BY SAND.

· 38 ·

THE GRAPHITE IN YOUR PENCIL IS MADE FROM THE SAME ELEMENT AS A DIAMOND.

Both are made entirely of carbon, but have different chemical structures.

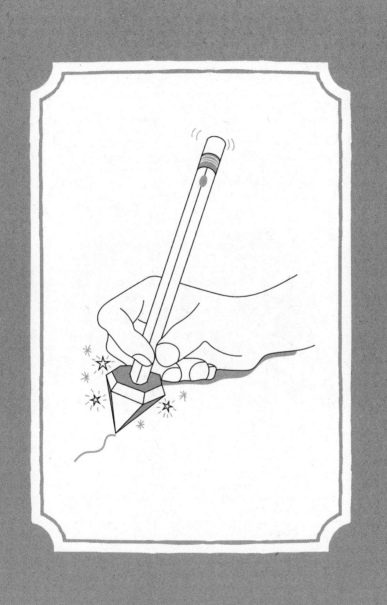

• 39 •

THE SMALLEST DESERT IN THE WORLD IS FOUND IN YUKON, CANADA.

Known as the Carcross Desert, it
measures just 1 square mile (2.6
square kilometers)!

40. **TANZANIA'S LAKE NATRON CONTAINS MASSIVE AMOUNTS OF SODIUM CARBONATE—A SUBSTANCE USED BY THE EGYPTIANS DURING THE MUMMIFICATION PROCESS.**

When animals in and around the lake die, the sodium carbonate coats their bodies, preserving them and giving them a spooky, stonelike appearance.

41. **A "GRAVITY HILL" IS A UNIQUE PHENOMENON WHERE THE SURROUNDING FEATURES CREATE AN OPTICAL ILLUSION, MAKING IT APPEAR THAT A HILL SLOPING DOWNHILL IS ACTUALLY SLOPING UPHILL.**

This can make it look like water is running uphill!

42. **VERYOVKINA CAVE IN THE NATION OF GEORGIA IS THE DEEPEST KNOWN CAVE IN THE WORLD, REACHING A DEPTH OF 7,257 FEET (2,212 METERS)—WELL OVER A MILE.**

43. **DURING FOGGY WEATHER, YOU MIGHT EXPERIENCE THE PHENOMENON KNOWN AS A "BROCKEN SPECTRE," WHERE A PERSON'S SHADOW IS REFLECTED AND MAGNIFIED, TAKING ON A GIANT, GHOSTLIKE FORM.**

44. **DURING WORLD WAR II, THE BRITISH CAME UP WITH A UNIQUE WAY TO CLEAR FOG FROM AIRFIELD RUNWAYS: THEY LINED THE EDGES WITH GASOLINE AND SET IT ON FIRE, "BURNING OFF" THE FOG TO IMPROVE VISIBILITY.**

45. RECENT RESEARCH INDICATES THAT THE GRAND CANYON IS NOT SIX MILLION YEARS OLD, AS SCIENTISTS INITIALLY BELIEVED—IN FACT, ITS FORMATION MAY HAVE STARTED AS FAR BACK AS 70 MILLION YEARS AGO.

46. IMPRESSIVE AS THE GRAND CANYON IS, IT IS NOT THE DEEPEST CANYON IN THE WORLD.

That honor belongs to the Yarlung Tsangpo Grand Canyon in Tibet, which reaches an astonishing depth of 19,714 feet (6,009 meters).

47. THE "GREAT UNCONFORMITY" REFERS TO AN UNEXPLAINED TIME GAP IN EARTH'S ROCK RECORD FROM WHICH NO ROCKS ARE PRESERVED.

While small gaps are not uncommon, the Great Unconformity is unique because of the large span of time it covers and the fact that it can be observed across the entire globe.

48. THE DEADLIEST TYPE OF WEATHER ISN'T A HURRICANE OR TORNADO: IT'S HEAT.

Extreme heat kills more humans across the globe than any other weather.

49. THANKS TO THE WARMING CLIMATE, THE EARTH IS NOW LOSING AN ESTIMATED 1.2 TRILLION TONS (1.1 TRILLION METRIC TONS) OF ICE EACH YEAR.

· 50 ·

THROUGHOUT HISTORY, SALT HAS BEEN AN INCREDIBLY VALUABLE RESOURCE.

Roman soldiers were sometimes paid in salt—in fact, the word "salary" comes from the Latin word for salt.

• 51 •

BOUVET ISLAND IS THE MOST REMOTE ISLAND IN THE WORLD.

The nearest island is almost 1,000 miles (1,609 kilometers) away—and the nearest inhabited island is even farther.

52. "SAILING STONES" ARE A PHENOMENON IN WHICH ROCKS APPEAR TO MOVE ON THEIR OWN ACROSS THE DESERT.

In reality, small amounts of ice are responsible for the movement.

53. "PANGAEA" ISN'T THE ONLY SUPERCONTINENT IN EARTH'S HISTORY.

Roughly 500 million years before Pangaea, there was Rodinia, a supercontinent with what is now North America at its center.

54. GRAVITY ISN'T THE SAME ALL ACROSS THE EARTH: THERE ARE PLACES WHERE GRAVITY ACTS STRONGER OR WEAKER (ALTITUDE IS USUALLY THE PRIMARY FACTOR).

55. THE LARGEST TORNADO OUTBREAK IN HISTORY HAPPENED IN THE UNITED STATES IN 2011.

There were 360 tornadoes recorded over a four-day period—a record for a single continuous outbreak.

56. THE LARGEST HAILSTONE EVER RECORDED WAS A MASSIVE 8 INCHES (20 CENTIMETERS) ACROSS AND WEIGHED NEARLY TWO POUNDS (ONE KILOGRAM).

57. LIGHTNING FLASHES ARE USUALLY INSTANTANEOUS, BUT NOT ALWAYS.

In 2020, scientists observed a lightning flash in South America that lasted an incredible 17 seconds.

58. THE LARGEST CONFIRMED IMPACT CRATER ON EARTH IS THE VREDEFORT IMPACT STRUCTURE IN SOUTH AFRICA.

When it first formed, the crater is believed to have been between 100 miles and 200 miles (between 161 kilometers and 322 kilometers) across, though erosion has taken its toll over time.

59. THERE HAVE BEEN AT LEAST FIVE "MASS EXTINCTION EVENTS" IN EARTH'S HISTORY, AND SCIENTISTS BELIEVE THAT WE MAY BE HEADING INTO A SIXTH.

60. TECHNICALLY, MOUNT EVEREST IS NOT THE TALLEST MOUNTAIN IN THE WORLD.

Measured from base to summit, Hawaii's Mauna Kea volcano is taller, but it doesn't reach as far above sea level.

61. THERE ARE AN ESTIMATED 1,350 ACTIVE VOLCANOES ON THE PLANET RIGHT NOW.

62. "EXPLODING LAKES" ARE A THING.

These lakes are prone to natural disasters known as limnic eruptions, in which dissolved carbon dioxide suddenly emerges from the depths and forms a gas cloud that suffocates any nearby animals—including humans.

• 63 •

EARTH'S MAGNETIC POLES REVERSE EVERY SO OFTEN—USUALLY EVERY 300,000 YEARS TO 400,000 YEARS.

It probably won't happen anytime soon, though.

· 64 ·

CONTINENTAL DRIFT HAPPENS ALL AROUND THE WORLD, BUT AUSTRALIA'S TECTONIC PLATE IS MOVING SO QUICKLY THAT GPS SERVICES NEED TO BE REGULARLY UPDATED TO COMPENSATE FOR ITS MOVEMENT!

65. THE YELLOWSTONE CALDERA IS A SUPERVOLCANO LOCATED IN WYOMING'S YELLOWSTONE NATIONAL PARK.

It last erupted roughly 640,000 years ago, and while it isn't expected to erupt again anytime soon, the consequences will be catastrophic when it eventually does.

66. MANY SCIENTISTS BELIEVE THAT A SUPERVOLCANO ERUPTION IN INDONESIA APPROXIMATELY 74,000 YEARS AGO MAY HAVE RESULTED IN A 1,000-YEAR-LONG PERIOD OF LOWER TEMPERATURES AND CAUSED A SIGNIFICANT DROP IN THE PLANET'S HUMAN POPULATION.

67. ROUGHLY 75% OF THE WORLD'S VOLCANOES ARE LOCATED IN THE "RING OF FIRE" THAT CIRCLES THE PACIFIC OCEAN.

Approximately 90% of the world's earthquakes also occur in this region.

68. SAND AND DUST CAN TRAVEL A LONG WAY: SAND CLOUDS FROM THE SAHARA DESERT HAVE BEEN KNOWN TO MAKE THEIR WAY ACROSS THE ATLANTIC OCEAN, ALL THE WAY TO AMERICA!

69. THE EARTH IS CONSTANTLY HUMMING. SEISMOMETERS, WHICH ARE USED TO MEASURE EARTHQUAKES, MEASURE A SLIGHT PULSE EVERY SIX SECONDS, CAUSED BY THE OCEAN WAVES CRASHING DOWN AROUND THE WORLD.

70. ROUGHLY 40% OF THE GLOBAL POPULATION LIVES WITHIN 62 MILES (100 KILOMETERS) OF THE COAST.

71. ABOUT 2% OF THE RESIDENTS OF TAOS, NEW MEXICO, HAVE REPORTED HEARING A CONSTANT, LOW-FREQUENCY HUM SINCE THE 1990S.

It appears to have a range of about 30 miles (48 kilometers), and scientists are not sure what is causing it.

72. A "LEAP SECOND" IS ADDED TO EARTH'S COORDINATED UNIVERSAL TIME (UTC) EVERY 18 MONTHS OR SO, TO ACCOUNT FOR SMALL CHANGES IN THE PLANET'S ROTATION.

73. THE MOST REMOTE LOCATION ON EARTH IS A SPOT IN THE PACIFIC OCEAN KNOWN AS "POINT NEMO."

It is so far from any human activity that the astronauts on the International Space Station are sometimes the closest human beings.

74. PHOTONS DO NOT EXPERIENCE TIME.

Because photons—light particles—travel at the speed of light, they do not perceive the passage of time at all. In fact, a photon would not even be aware that the rest of the universe exists. At the speed of light, it would have no way to perceive it.

• 75 •

"RINGING ROCKS" (ALSO KNOWN AS "SONOROUS STONES") ARE MUSICAL ROCKS THAT RING LIKE A BELL WHEN STRUCK.

For some reason, they are mostly found in the Pennsylvania and New Jersey areas.

76. BALL LIGHTNING IS AN AS-YET UNEXPLAINED PHENOMENON IN WHICH LUMINOUS BALLS OF VARYING SIZE APPEAR, EXPLODE, AND LEAVE A SULFUR-LIKE SMELL IN THEIR WAKE.

77. OXYGEN IS DIATOMIC, MEANING THAT AN OXYGEN MOLECULE (O_2) IS MADE UP OF TWO OXYGEN ATOMS.

Add a third oxygen atom, and you get O_3: ozone. Funny what adding one atom can do—O_2 is one of the building blocks of life, while O_3 is harmful to humans!

78. KENTUCKY'S MAMMOTH CAVE IS THE LONGEST KNOWN CAVE SYSTEM ON EARTH.

More than 400 miles (644 kilometers) of caves have already been explored, and scientists estimate that there may still be another 600 miles (966 kilometers) to discover!

79. A FULL ROTATION OF THE EARTH DOESN'T ACTUALLY TAKE 24 HOURS—IT TAKES 23 HOURS, 56 MINUTES, AND 4 SECONDS.

The remaining 4 minutes are accounted for by the Earth's movement around the sun.

80. THE SKY CAN SOMETIMES TURN GREEN BEFORE A THUNDERSTORM, AND NO ONE IS ENTIRELY SURE WHY.

81. TRUE OR FALSE: LIGHTNING NEVER STRIKES THE SAME PLACE TWICE.

False. Actually, lightning strikes the same place all the time. For example, the Empire State Building gets struck by lightning at least 25 times per year.

82. TRUE OR FALSE: LIGHTNING IS HOTTER THAN THE SURFACE OF THE SUN.

True. Lightning can heat the air around it to temperatures of over 50,000 degrees Fahrenheit (27,760 degrees Celsius). Believe it or not, that's roughly five times hotter than the surface of the sun.

83. TRUE OR FALSE: THE TOP OF MOUNT EVEREST IS THE POINT FARTHEST FROM EARTH'S CENTER.

False. Mount Everest is the highest point above sea level, but the Earth isn't a perfect sphere; it bulges slightly at its equator. As a result, the peak of Chimborazo, a dormant volcano located in Ecuador, is the farthest point from the center of the Earth.

84. TRUE OR FALSE: EARTH ACTUALLY HAS TWO NORTH POLES.

True. There is the geographic North Pole and the magnetic North Pole. The geographic North Pole is the fixed location where all lines of longitude converge, while the magnetic North Pole shifts with Earth's magnetic field.

· 85 ·

TRUE OR FALSE: THE RECORD FOR THE GREATEST TEMPERATURE CHANGE IN A SINGLE 24-HOUR PERIOD IS MORE THAN 100 DEGREES FAHRENHEIT (56 DEGREES CELSIUS).

True. It's actually an astonishing 103 degrees Fahrenheit (57 degrees Celsius). In 1972, temperatures in Loma, Montana, rose from -54 degrees Fahrenheit (-48 degrees Celsius) to 49 degrees Fahrenheit (9 degrees Celsius) over the course of a day.

• 86 •

TRUE OR FALSE: WHEN LIGHTNING STRIKES SAND, IT CREATES GLASS.

True. It creates a tube-shaped sculpture of glass in the ground. It doesn't look like much at first, since the outside of the glass is coated in burnt sand.

87. TRUE OR FALSE: WE HAVE NEVER EXPERIENCED A MAGNITUDE 10 EARTHQUAKE.

True. The most powerful earthquake in history was the 1960 Valdivia earthquake in Chile, which was a 9.5 on the Richter scale.

88. TRUE OR FALSE: THE SOUTH POLE IS COLDER THAN THE NORTH POLE.

True. You might think they would be the same temperature, but no: the South Pole is actually much colder than the North Pole. This is largely due to the fact that Antarctica is both higher and dryer than the largely ocean-based Arctic.

89. TRUE OR FALSE: WHAT WE CONSIDER "SEA LEVEL" HAS CHANGED CONSIDERABLY OVER TIME.

True. At different times throughout history, it has been both hundreds of feet higher and hundreds of feet lower than it is today.

90. TRUE OR FALSE: DIAMONDS ARE THE RAREST GEMS.

False. In fact, diamonds aren't particularly rare at all. But high-quality diamonds are—which is what makes them so expensive (that, and a tightly controlled market).

91. TRUE OR FALSE: "ASIAMERICA" IS THE NAME GIVEN TO THE PREDICTED SUPERCONTINENT THAT WILL FORM WHEN ASIA AND THE AMERICAS COLLIDE IN 200 MILLION YEARS.

False. But the truth isn't any more imaginative: scientists refer to the future landmass as "Amasia."

92. TRUE OR FALSE: SOME SCIENTISTS BELIEVE THAT DURING AT LEAST ONE POINT IN HISTORY, THE EARTH WAS COMPLETELY COVERED IN ICE.

True. The "Snowball Earth" theory is just that—a theory—but there is a decent amount of evidence that supports it.

93. TRUE OR FALSE: THE SPEED OF EARTH'S ROTATION IS DICTATED BY HOW FAST ITS CORE ROTATES.

False. The Earth's core does not rotate at the same rate as the rest of the Earth—in fact, scientists have recently found that the core may be slowing down and possibly even reversing direction.

94. TRUE OR FALSE: THE APPALACHIAN MOUNTAINS WERE ONCE AS TALL AS THE HIMALAYAS.

True. At least, we think it's true. The Appalachians are very old and have been worn down over time, whereas the Himalayas are still (relatively) young. Scientists believe that the Appalachians may have once been at least as tall as the Himalayas are today.

95. TRUE OR FALSE: THE EARTH TRAVELS AROUND THE SUN AT ROUGHLY 1,000 MPH (1,609 KMH).

False. The Earth moves around the sun at a blistering speed of 67,000 mph (107,826 kmh). However, it rotates on its axis at 1,000 mph (1,609 kmh).

• 96 •

TRUE OR FALSE: FLORIDA WAS ONCE PART OF AFRICA.

True. Amazingly, this is a real fact! The Florida peninsula originally formed as a part of northwestern Africa.

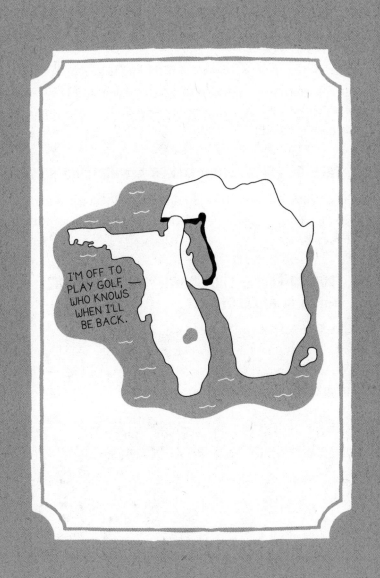

97. TRUE OR FALSE: THE "EYE OF THE STORM" IS A MYTH—ACTUALLY, THE CENTER OF A STORM IS WHERE IT IS WINDIEST.

False. Nope—the "eye of the storm" lives up to its reputation! It can appear calm and sunny in the eye...just don't be fooled into going outside. The area immediately around the eye has some of the harshest conditions of all.

98. TRUE OR FALSE: WIND MAKES A WHISTLING NOISE.

False. Wind itself is silent—its trademark whipping and whistling noises only happen when it comes into contact with a physical object.

99. TRUE OR FALSE: THE SNOWIEST PLACE IN THE WORLD IS ANTARCTICA.

False. Believe it or not, the snowiest place on Earth isn't Antarctica. It's not the North Pole either. No, the snowiest place on Earth is Aomori City, Japan, which receives an average of 312 inches (792 centimeters) of snow per year.

100. TRUE OR FALSE: THE AVERAGE HURRICANE RELEASES MORE ENERGY THAN AN ATOMIC BOMB.

True. In fact, it releases MUCH more energy than an atomic bomb—10,000 times more, according to NASA.

Acknowledgments

This book required an extensive amount of research, and I want to call out some of the sources that helped me the most in this wonderful journey of discovery. A warm thank-you to:

- *Smithsonian* magazine
- National Geographic
- *Nature*
- Discovery
- *Scientific American*
- *Popular Mechanics*
- Atlas Obscura
- National Library of Medicine
- The National Aeronautics and Space Administration (NASA)
- National Oceanic and Atmospheric Administration (NOAA)
- National Audubon Society
- Ocean Conservancy
- People for the Ethical Treatment of Animals (PETA)
- Guinness World Records
- Phys.org
- Science.org
- Wikipedia (which was often an excellent starting point)
- Snopes (to bust some of the peskier myths)
- …and countless others

And finally, a thank-you to the many denizens of social media, including X (formerly Twitter) and Reddit. Your facts weren't always correct, but even the wrong ones sent me down fun and fruitful rabbit holes. Please never stop posting.

ABOUT SHANE CARLEY

Shane Carley lives deep in the woods of Western Massachusetts, hammering away on his keyboard between trips to walk the dog and feed the chickens. When he isn't researching obscure trivia to include in his next book, he is probably experimenting with new cocktail recipes for his highly popular Home Bartender book series. In his other life, Shane spearheads content development for an award-winning public relations firm, where he helps ensure his clients' words do not, in fact, sound like *bull$#*t*.

ABOUT CIDER MILL PRESS BOOK PUBLISHERS

Good ideas ripen with time. From seed to harvest, Cider Mill Press brings fine reading, information, and entertainment together between the covers of its creatively crafted books. Our Cider Mill bears fruit twice a year, publishing a new crop of titles each spring and fall.

"Where Good Books Are Ready for Press"
501 Nelson Place
Nashville, Tennessee 37214
cidermillpress.com